The Laws of SUCCESS

The Laws of SUCCESS

Sterling W. Sill

There is a law, irrevocably decreed
in heaven before the foundations of this world,
upon which all blessings are predicated—

And when we obtain any blessing
from God, it is by obedience to that law upon
which it is predicated.

—D&C 130:20-21

Published by
Deseret Book Company
Salt Lake City, Utah
1977

Library of Congress Card Catalog No. 75-18818
ISBN 0-87747-556-3

CONTENTS

1 The Law 1
2 The Lawgiver 7
3 The Law of Abundance 13
4 The Law of Advantage 19
5 The Law of Appreciation 22
6 The Law of Arrested Development 26
7 The Law of the Boomerang 31
8 The Law of Chance 34
9 The Law of Compensation 37
10 The Law of Concentration 43
11 The Law of Conditioned Responses 48
12 The Law of Consequences 51
13 The Law of Courage 55
14 The Law of Ego Recognition 59
15 The Law of Elegance 63
16 The Law of Evidence 67
17 The Law of Exaggeration 72
18 The Law of Example 78
19 The Law of Experience 84
20 The Law of Fear 89
21 The Law of Financial Respectability 94
22 The Law of Free Agency 100

23	The Law of Fusion	103
24	The Law of Glad Tidings	105
25	The Law of Gravity-Up	109
26	The Law of Growth	113
27	The Law of Health	116
28	The Law of the Hurdle	121
29	The Law of Hypochondria	125
30	The Law of Idleness	128
31	The Law of Instincts	131
32	The Law of Love	135
33	The Law of Loyalty	140
34	The Law of Maturity	144
35	The Law of Modification	149
36	The Law of Objectives 153	153
37	The Law of Positive Statement	158
38	The Law of Probability	161
39	The Law of Reason	166
40	The Law of Self-Control	170
41	The Law of Self-Deception	173
42	The Law of Self-Pity	178
43	The Law of Self-Supervision	181
44	The Law of the Split Personality	185
45	The Law of Symbols	189
46	The Laws of Teaching	194
47	The Law of Trifles	198
48	The Law of Vision	203
49	The Law of the Will	207
50	The Law of Words	210
	Index	215

1 The LAW

Some time ago, I heard the report of a discussion that had taken place between a university teacher of political science and a businessman with a strong religious avocation. The political science teacher said that politics and government should be the most important influence in our lives. The businessman, who had also had some political experience, said that *his* first allegiance was to the church. Then there was some discussion about priorities of these two great areas in our lives and where one's primary allegiance ought to be placed.

The political science teacher pointed out that good, solid government is the real basis for success in every field, including religion, for no activity prospers in the face of misrule, disorder, or anarchy. He noted that freedom of religion and real worship cannot exist at their best without righteous government, and even one's own personal devotions, his personal security, and his peace of mind can't proceed very far until he gets his basic politics straightened out. We know of many situations in which political persecution has destroyed the functions of religion, or a political leader has said to those seeking redress of grievances, "Your cause is just but I can do nothing for you."

There are also many forms of government that try to bind the consciences of men, and religion does not prosper under an evil dictatorship that attempts to make slaves out of its subjects and to dictate to them in matters of the mind and spirit. Certainly government and those who are responsible for government have a very important place in the life of every individual.

It is the duty of government to protect life and property, maintain order, guarantee fairness, and see that sedition, rebellion, or other evils do not interfere with freedom of religion and the natural God-given rights of each human being. Government even reaches into our family lives to regulate marriage and divorce, child welfare and neglect.

On the other hand, the businessman reasoned that his religious beliefs should take preference over his loyalty to the government. He argued that unless a person is imbued with the fundamental principles of religion and righteousness, no government can long prosper; many great civilizations have failed and disappeared from the earth because they have taken God and the church out of their lives and out of their government.

It seems to me that each one of us should have some strong arguments for ourselves on all sides of this proposition. It may be that each one is important. Even apart from the church, religion should permeate everything that we do in government, in business, in human relations, and particularly in our families. Governments should also foster the influences of real godliness. The value of both the church and the state can be judged by the kinds of laws they promote for the benefit of the people. Certainly the laws of the land should be compatible with the laws of God, and our United States Constitution provides that the government shall make no law that interferes with the freedom of religion. On the other hand, the freedom of religion must not interfere with nor infringe upon the rights of others.

The church is a divine institution organized by God himself for the benefit of man. It is responsible for teaching the great principles of truth upon which our eternal salvation depends. God himself has given many laws and commandments to regulate our lives. A great scripture says that governments were established by God for the benefit of man and that he will hold us responsible for our acts in relationship thereto. That is, the government is a divine institution, though it has a little different set of responsibilities from those of the church. The family is also a divine institution. And each of these great establishments has over the centuries been the focal point for the attack of evil.

Jesus himself was crucified, and each of the twelve apostles, with one exception, had a violent death imposed upon him. Isaiah described some of the problems of disobedience, persecution, and apostasy when he said, ". . . they have transgressed the laws, changed the ordinance, broken the everlasting covenant." (Isaiah 24:5.)

There are other forces continually at work against law and order, and many kinds of governments, including democratic, dictatorship, socialistic, and communistic. Over the centuries, many governments have risen and fallen because of their violation of the laws of God.

In our times, there are many attempts from both the outside and the inside to destroy the government, tear down the establishment, discredit our finest social traditions, and cause the deterioration of the family. We have a great need to separate the church and the state. The church has the difficult job of teaching truth and righteousness, building character, and preparing the souls of people not only for their place in the government and society of this life, but also for that life which lies beyond our mortal boundaries. The government has the responsibility for making and enforcing laws for the protection and benefit of all the people, religious or nonreligious. Both share one function: to make us successful and happy for both here and hereafter. The job of each, most simply stated, is to help us to honor, love, and obey the law—the laws of the land and the laws of the Lord.

The Lord said, "I will put my law into their hearts, and in their minds will I write them." (Hebrews 10:16.) It seems to me that this puts the Lord into the role of being our greatest political officer, as well as the head of the church. We are told that during the millennium he will establish a perfect theocracy upon this earth, with himself as the head of the government as well as the head of the church. The church and the state will then be combined, and he will rule forever, not only as Lord of lords, but also as King of kings.

The function of making and enforcing the law is given to senates, legislatures, parliaments, dictators, and individual citizens. A father recently reported that during their family home evening he was telling his family how very important it is in their lives for them to keep all of the commandments. One of his daughters said, "Daddy, how many commandments are there?" And so for the next family home evening, they took up the project of trying to enumerate the commandments. They included the Ten Commandments, the law of tithing, and the Word of Wisdom. They also included the important laws given by the Savior when a lawyer asked him, "Master, which is the greatest commandment in the law? Jesus said unto him, Thou shalt love the Lord thy God with all thy heart, and with all thy soul, and with all thy mind. This is the first and great commandment. And the second is like unto it, Thou shalt love thy neighbour as thyself. On these two commandments hang all the law and the prophets." (Matthew 22:35-40.)

The primary function of every individual is to discover and obey all the laws. The doctor, to be effective, must learn the laws of medicine. The successful agriculturalist must learn the laws of farming. He should know that if he plants his seed in a good seedbed and practices the laws having to do with fertilization, cultivation, and irrigation, and also has some knowledge of weed and insect control, he may hope to be a successful farmer. To effectively counsel his many clients, a lawyer may need thousands of law books; he must make himself familiar with all of the laws affecting his clients' welfare.

There are many laws that have not been written down or even discovered, and yet we must be subject to them. An old adage says, "Ignorance of the law excuses no one." If we do not know that the highway speed limit is fifty-five miles an hour and in our ignorance we travel eighty-five miles an hour, we must be ready to pay the penalty. If one has never learned that strychnine can kill, he places himself in great danger.

The apostle Paul said to the Romans, "For as many as have sinned without the law shall also perish without the law. . . ." (Romans 2:12.) Our success depends upon how effective we are as discoverers and followers of all of the laws that will influence our success or failure. Benjamin Franklin discovered some of the laws of electricity. Newton discovered the law of gravity. Galileo discovered the law of falling bodies. Einstein discovered the law of relativity. Kepler discovered the law of planetary motion. There are laws of heredity, laws of learning, laws of business success, laws of motion, laws of holiness. Every great principle of truth, righteousness, and success is underwritten by fundamental, immutable laws.

The great multiplicity of the laws that govern our lives may at first seem overwhelming. However, we are not left entirely without assistance in understanding those laws that we must obey. Again, the Lord has said, "I will put my laws into their hearts, and in their minds will I write them." (Hebrews 10:16.) One of the most fantastic of all of God's creations is a conscience that has not been abused or distorted.

After our first parents had eaten the fruit from the tree of knowledge of good and evil, God said of them, "Behold, the man is now become as one of us, to know good and evil. . . ." (Genesis 3:22.) That ability has been transmitted to all of the posterity of our first parents on a kind of instinctive basis, and it is still true that the right kind of discrimination between right and wrong will help make men and women become as God. However, we need to think about it and to make decisions about issues and take action on our decisions. One of the greatest benefits of our lives is to be masters or doctors of the law. We ought to have an understanding of those fundamental principles and truths that can give our lives great significance and joy.

It was with this in mind that this book has been titled *The Laws of Success.* If you will read the chapters carefully and take note of the many places where the principles discussed may be advantageously applied, your prosperity will be increased in many areas of your life. In addition, you will also be aware of other necessary laws so that you can write your own book describing for your own personal benefit some of the powerful laws that you may not presently be using. Everyone who is working toward that ultimate goal of eternal accomplishment ought to have the thrill of discovering for himself more of life's universal laws of success.

2 The LAWGIVER

We who live upon the earth are indebted to a great many people for a great many things. We think of Hippocrates as the father of medicine, and from his humble beginnings a great science has developed that gives us a maximum of life and health and strength. Abraham was the father of the faithful. We think of Thomas A. Edison as the great genius who lighted our world and transformed it by giving it power. Luther Burbank gave us many improved varieties of plants and fruits and flowers. The Wright brothers pioneered in aviation, and Henry Ford was one of the great pioneers of the automobile industry. Albert Einstein developed the theory of relativity. We are grateful to the master painters, composers, authors, inventors, musicians, and workers who have so greatly enlightened and enriched our world. But probably the greatest benefactors of our lives are those who have given us our laws to live by.

God, the Creator of our earth, is the one who has given us life, but even life itself would have very little value if we did not also have objectives, self-discipline, law, and order to make it meaningful and by which we might bring about our own happiness, success, and progress. And it may be that God made his greatest contribution to us as the supreme lawgiver of the universe.

As we turn back the calendar to watch the progress of creation, we read how "the earth was without form, and void; and darkness was upon the face of the deep." (Genesis 1:2.) There are, of course, many kinds of darkness, including mental darkness, spiritual darkness, physical darkness, and moral darkness. There are many conditions that we can't see clearly, and others that we don't understand, and many that we just don't care about. We might try to contemplate human life upon an earth that was without form and void and where darkness reigned supreme throughout nature. In our individual lives, we might also try to imagine a life in which we had no purpose, no ambition, no education, no understanding, no objectives, and no law. Under these circumstances, we might be far worse off than the animals, who are governed by instinct from which they may not deviate. Only to man did God say, "Thou mayest choose for thyself." (Moses 3:17.)

We might go back in imagination and wonder what we might have been like without laws. Suppose we were to feel again that brooding, unbroken darkness that covered the earth and try to understand what it must have been like when in the beginning God gave his first law, saying, "Let there be light." (Genesis 1:3.) God did a great many other interesting things. The record says, "And the spirit of God moved upon the face of the waters." (Genesis 1:2.) He moved upon our lives and gave us our instincts and our intellect. He became the lawgiver of the universe, with us as his primary beneficiaries. He established the laws of light and heat and gravity, of centrifugal force, and of electricity. He ordained the rotation of the planets and the laws governing the seasons. He invented seeds and growth, death and eternal life—all in our interests.

Standing next to God, some of the other great people of our earth have been lawgivers. In the early days after the flood, one of the kings of Babylon was Hammurabi, who ruled in Babylon several hundred years before the days of Moses and who helped to establish that great code of laws on which the famous Babylonian empire was built. This great empire finally fell because the people failed to follow the laws by which their great power had been established.

Because they forsook the law, the prophet Jeremiah said of them, "And Babylon shall become heaps, a dwellingplace for dragons, an astonishment, and an hissing, without an inhabitant." (Jeremiah 51:37.) "Her cities are a desolation, a dry land, and a wilderness, a land wherein no man dwelleth, neither doth any son of man pass thereby." (Jeremiah 51:43.) "Thus saith the Lord of hosts; The broad walls of Babylon shall be utterly broken, and her high gates shall be burned with fire; and the people shall labour in vain. . . ." (Jeremiah 51:58.) "Then shalt thou say, O Lord, thou hast spoken against this place, to cut it off, that none shall remain in it, neither man nor beast, but that it shall be desolate for ever." (Jeremiah 51:62.)

That is a very accurate description of the present site of the once proud mistress of the world, and this is also similar to what happens to us as individuals when we forsake the God-given laws of our lives.

One of the greatest contributions ever made to the world was the one made by Moses in his role as the lawgiver for ancient Israel. During the period that the law was given, God himself came down to the top of Mount Sinai and called Moses up to meet him. Then God gave Moses the great rules of conduct by which, if obeyed, this earth might become God's paradise. These great laws, known as the Ten Commandments, furnish the fundamental basis on which all order, progress, success, happiness, and beauty must rest.

The council of heaven was devoted largely to a discussion of the law and order that should obtain upon this earth when we would live here. Long before the earth was created, God had made an everlasting commitment to the fact that men should be free and their lives judged according to their works. When that proposal was contested and Lucifer rebelled against God, there was a war in heaven. The greatest lawgiver who has ever lived upon this earth was the Son of God, who in the council of heaven was appointed to be the Savior of the world and the Redeemer of mankind. In the meridian of time he came to earth and established the laws of the gospel, those great principles which, if followed, would bring about our eternal exaltation. Everything in our life depends upon our obedience to the laws and ordinances on which our eternal salvation is based.

One of the greatest of all the lawgivers in the world was George Washington, who became known as the father of his country. He led the colonial forces in winning American independence and freedom. He was the leading spirit in that great group of men raised up by God to write the Constitution of the nation where the Church of Christ was to be restored, a set of laws that gave America its start toward its destiny. This nation under God was also given the all-important mission of keeping freedom, righteousness, and human dignity alive in the world. It is thought that no other man among all the great men of colonial times could have guided America to its high degree of success.

One of the important occupations of the world is that of our lawyers, whose job is to study the law, to propose new laws, to do away with poor laws, and to help everybody obey the law. In a little different sense, every one of us ought to be a lawyer and a lawgiver. George Washington, Moses, Hammurabi, or even God himself cannot solve our problems without our help. No one can do our thinking for us. No one can build our attitudes for us, and no one can provide our own disciplines. We ourselves must take the lead in being our own lawgivers, our own judges, our own policemen.

I know a great salesman who in the process of building up his own ability wrote a series of articles on what he conceived the laws of great salesmanship to be. He wrote down all that he could discover about those sales principles that he at first only partially understood, and he thereby made himself somewhat of an authority on the laws of successful salesmanship.

We might also write down our own understanding of the laws and the advantages of having objectives, using our will power, and developing our expression. The apostle James said that "if any be a hearer of the word, and not a doer, he is like unto a man beholding his natural face in a glass: For he beholdeth himself, and goeth his way, and straightway forgetteth what manner of man he was." (James 1:23-24.) In a similar manner, we sometimes think of the important laws governing life and success, but because we are inclined to be hearers only and not doers, we go our way and forget the laws that we are supposed to remember.

An applicant for a master's thesis is required to major in a special area of study and then do some original thinking, research, and homework, so that he can write an informative and beneficial thesis about his subject. This helps the writer and the reader. However, it is also a law that the teacher always learns more than the student, and the one who researches the law and writes down how to utilize its benefits will be its greatest beneficiary. The extra light generated and the extra enthusiasm involved when we do our homework well can help anyone to be a master salesman. The same procedure can also help to make us masters in the greater occupation of life itself.

The salesman mentioned above had previously been a farmer, and he knew what would happen if he failed to understand or practice the fundamental laws of farming. If he planted his corn in the chill of the December blizzard, he could not expect the harvest that might come if he were to plant his corn in the warmth of the May sunshine. Now suppose that each one of us were to conduct a similar kind of study of ourselves and our work. Suppose we were to write our own book of laws for successful living. It would be of little actual consequence whether our occupation is law or medicine or selling or life.

We might ask ourselves such questions as what do we think about the Golden Rule, or honesty, or fairness, and then require ourselves to give well-thought-out, practical, written answers that we are wholeheartedly committed to follow. Just as the scriptures are brief on some of the most important questions on which we need answers, so we need to expand our thinking and make sure that we fill in all the blank spaces so we may see the entire picture as it applies to us. This can be done in part by thoughtful, prayerful study and consideration.

Suppose we write down our own ideas and applications of the Golden Rule, or the Lord's Prayer, or the Sermon on the Mount. Or suppose we develop our own appreciation of the spirit of following the strait and narrow way or the philosophy of doing more than we get paid for, as illustrated in the Master's story of the second mile. We can learn a great deal by what we read. These ideas may be stamped more deeply into our minds when we think about them, write them down, and practice them.

Ideas and principles have great value. They are what we think about and believe in. But even more important are laws, because they outline what we must actually do to develop our own success. They are the ideas and principles that we are willing to put into actual working practice. God is the lawgiver of the universe, and under him we have had such men as Moses, Hammurabi, and George Washington, who have helped to write some of the constitutions and laws by which our lives and our governments may grow and flourish. Houses of congress, our courts, and our government leaders are concerned largely with the making and administering of the law, but none of these have great value to us without our own support. And so we nominate ourselves to be lawgivers, to take the great principles of the gospel, the laws of the land, the laws of success, the laws of health, and make them operative in our program of administering all the affairs of our own lives.

3 The Law of ABUNDANCE

Suppose you had a son whom you loved very much and that you had surrounded him with every opportunity and all good things. He could have all the education he wished. The medical knowledge is available that, if followed, would give him a strong body and a clear mind. He could develop personality, courage, industry, and leadership to his heart's content. All of the best things would be available to him in the greatest abundance. Can you conceive of placing any limit on him as long as this abundance was in his interest?

But after all of this opportunity, suppose your son showed himself to be unworthy, unkempt, without education, without personality, without vision or understanding, half-starved physically, mentally, and spiritually. How would you feel?

Isn't that just about our situation? Think of the lavish abundance with which creation surrounds us. Everything we could possibly wish for has been placed within our easy reach. It was certainly intended that everyone who wished it should have an abundance. There is enough and to spare. There is sufficient electricity in the water of a creek to furnish the power of a million slaves. There is almost enough atomic energy in the substance we could hold in one hand to run the world. If every person produced to his utmost and we did away with strikes, monopolies, crime, and waste, everyone could have his needs supplied many times over. Think of the lavishness of our natural resources: land, water, air, iron, coal deposits, forests, and oil. Think also of the resources in our own personality that lie buried and mostly unused.

Nature gives us everything in abundance and expects us to manifest that abundance in our lives. The Creator did not intend us to be scrubs, and certainly that is not the example that he sets for us. Only one millionth part of the sun's rays reach the planets that maintain life; the rest of its beams die in cold, empty space with nothing to reflect back heat and light. Think of the order, the efficiency, the regularity and dependability of the workings of the universe. Try to contemplate the efficiency and attitude of the mind that could produce such order and abundance. Do you suppose that the mind that brought into being worlds without number and all the wealth of creation intends us, his children, to be scrawny, uneducated, and underfed, deprived of the few things necessary to our happiness, or that he intends us to live in want, sickness, fear, ignorance, and insecurity?

Jesus said, "And all things, whatsoever ye shall ask in prayer, believing, ye shall receive." (Matthew 21:22.) "Give, and it shall be given unto you; good measure, pressed down, and shaken together, and running over. . . ." (Luke 6:38.)

There are no signs of any limitation mentioned here.

Think how lavishly nature rewards us for the things we do in a material way. If we plant one bushel of potato seed in the ground, we can get back sixty bushels of potatoes in return. A single potato carried to England by Sir Walter Raleigh in the sixteenth century multiplied itself in food for millions. A single tomato seed can multiply itself a million times in one year. Ten forests can come out of one acorn. Plant a pound of onion seed and we may reap ten tons of onions. One twig from an apple tree planted in the ground may become a great tree, producing foliage and blossoms and fragrance and fruit not just one year, but for many years, multiplied many, many times. The two eggs that we intended to eat for breakfast tomorrow morning could be hatched into a pair of fowls and multiplied to cover the earth with poultry.

Is it likely we would be rewarded less in other areas of life? A little investment in character pays us back a millionfold. Every pound of energy we put into education for the development of initiative, resourcefulness, courage, industry, and personality, we get back multiplied manyfold. For every manifestation of faith as a grain of mustard seed, we are told we can move mountains; every determination that we put into life comes back to us fantastically multiplied.

Nature is rich, and it was intended that every man, woman, and child should be rich likewise. To be in want is a sin. Plutarch said that while poverty may not be dishonorable in itself, it is usually the manifestation of laziness, intemperance, carelessness, lack of planning, and lack of courage. In contrast, upon a person who is temperate, industrious, just, and valiant and who uses all of his virtues and develops a great, lofty mind and an active body, fortune will pour her whole cornucopia of wealth, honor, and worldly goods.

The essence of the law of abundance is that we must believe in abundance. We must think abundance. We must raise our sights for greater accomplishments and let no thought of failure or limitation enter our minds. We must think success and feel success and work for success. Our boundaries should be expanded. "Man was intended to be rich," said Emerson.

Most of us tend to underrate our own dignity, importance, and potentiality. It was certainly not intended that we live as slaves, beggars, or vagrants. There is no such thing as lack of opportunity. The important thing is to believe and then take the first step. Just to begin is to complete the first half of the job. Then if we work toward the goal with all our hearts, why should failure even be thought of? It was never intended that we should be poor or worried or unable to pay our bills when we are surrounded with an abundance merely for the asking.

But when we think fear and discouragement and failure, that's what we get. To take advantage of the law of abundance, we must think strength, think health, think riches. Our achievements today are but the sum total of our thoughts of yesterday. Whatever price we set upon ourselves, life will give it to us. If we visualize and emphasize our worries, our fears, and our negative attitudes, we live with and become saturated by them. We make them real by our practice of failure. If we control our thoughts, we can control our circumstances. There is scarcely a poor person who was not made poor by his own shortcomings or by the shortcomings of someone else. It is all wrong to be poor anyway.

We often see potentially great salesmen who give many reasons why they cannot succeed. They think they have a lack of ability, or they are worried because of finances. They fill their minds with negative thoughts. How foolish and shortsighted is such counsel! In the first place, it is not true. Most of the great accomplishments in the world have been made under tremendous difficulty.

Both Caesar and Napoleon were epileptics at the very time in their lives when they were making themselves the most powerful. Many people who are presently drawing disability benefits are in better shape than Julius Caesar was while he was conquering the world. John Milton wrote *Paradise Lost*, one of the world's greatest pieces of literature, while he was totally blind and living in complete poverty. George Washington won the American Revolution with even his own family set against him, and in spite of Valley Forge, where his soldiers went barefoot in the snow, without food and without equipment. Abraham Lincoln had to borrow money for his railroad ticket to go to Washington to give his inaugural address. What would have happened if in his poverty he had said, "I can't work because I'm worried"? He had no money, no possessions, few opportunities; yet he raised himself to be one of our greatest presidents because he thought positively and kept trying.

We should be very careful about what we think, because that's what we become. If we think we can't, we can't; if we think failure, we fail. On the other hand, persons of faith and vision usually do their best work when they know there is no retreat. They decide to fight instead of run, and that is a great moment in anyone's life. Necessity is still the mother of invention, but it is more than that. It builds desire and determination, and it develops vision. There is no incentive like necessity. A determined purpose cannot be stopped. The more you dam it, the more power is accumulated behind the dam, until it eventually sweeps everything before it. Nothing can stop us if we only believe. Walt Whitman said, "Nothing external to me has any power over me."

The only time we get into trouble is when we start to whine and cringe and alibi and say, "I can't work or believe because . . ." We allow ourselves to think negatively about competition and hard times; we allow our fears and worries to undermine our confidence; and we fail to reach out and help ourselves to the abundance with which we are surrounded.

Thoughts are energy; thoughts are magnets that attract to us the various things we think. The greatest shortcut to prosperity is to believe in it. Prosperity attracts; poverty repels. This is the operation of the law which says, "For whosoever hath, to him shall be given, and he shall have more abundance: but whosoever hath not, from him shall be taken away even that he hath." (Matthew 13:12.)

In one way, failure is like success. Both are "inside" jobs. People live in poverty and want because they are so wrapped up in their suffering that they give out thoughts of poverty and unhappiness. Thoughts attract in kind, and when we think poverty, nothing else is possible. All of our lives we have known in a vague sort of way that developing our faith, like getting money, is the result of earning it, but most of us never get a very good vision of that very powerful idea. Summed up, the result of all experience is that man gets back exactly what he gives out, except it is multiplied.

Many of us have eyes but don't see the great opportunities that are staring us in the face. The poor fellow who said "I hid my talent in the ground and have earned nothing" was not only afraid; he was also blind. Of course, the first and all-important thing is that we must know what we want. Before we can have our heart's desire, we must get clearly fixed in our mind's eye what we want and then concentrate all our attention on that one thing. Most of us struggle on in a vague sort of way, hoping that something may turn up, not knowing definitely what we expect. We usually waste enough energy to get us to our destination—if we only knew where we wanted to go. But like a drowning man, we fritter away our strength in futile struggle, threshing the air without direction, exhausting ourselves without getting anywhere. Most of us spend far more energy on the detours than on the main line.

Remember that nature is rich, and Creation intends that all shall have an abundance, good measure, pressed down, shaken together, filled up, and running over. All we need to do is obey the law of abundance.

> I bargained with life for a penny,
> Only to find dismayed
> That anything I had asked of life,
> Life would have paid.

4 The Law of ADVANTAGE

One of the most important differences between modern men and those of earlier periods is in the fact that modern men have invented and learned to use tools to make their work more effective. For example, a person whose large automobile may have a flat tire couldn't begin to lift up the front end of the vehicle by himself to change the tire, so he gets out of the trunk of the car a little tool that he calls a jack. He puts it under the front of his car, turns the crank to the jack, and, with almost no effort or strain, quickly lifts the entire end of the automobile into the air.

If one were to put a 500-pound weight on one end of a rope and a 150-pound man on the other end and suspend them in the air with a rope through a pulley, the weight would drop to the ground and crash the man into the pulley. But if this same rope were run through a block and tackle and again suspended in the air with the man on the end of the rope and the 500-pound weight on the block and tackle, this time the weight could be lifted up and the man lowered. By means of a simple lever, a man can lift several times more weight than he otherwise could. We call this ability to multiply our strength by the use of tools "mechanical advantage."

By another device, a man with a pump and some water might lift a great battleship over a mountain by means of locks constructed for that purpose. The battleship is sailed into the lower locks and water pumped in until the locks are full. The locks are arranged like stairs, and when the lock is full, the gates on the stair above are opened and the battleship floated in on the new and higher level; then the gates are closed behind it. When water is pumped up to the new level, the battleship is again lifted up, and the process is repeated.

Though the compartment in which the battleship floats may be only a hundred feet wide and the battleship ninety feet wide, the water can force the battleship up; and this simple process, if repeated enough times, could carry the battleship to the top of the mountain. Not only would it go up the mountain, but the same water, with almost no effort or pump, could be used to lower the battleship down the other side of the mountain. The jack and the block and tackle and the water and the lever may not have any power in themselves, but they can make giants out of ordinary men who learn to use them properly.

This law of advantage can be applied in other areas of our lives. For example, suppose a man buys a $10,000 family income insurance policy and pays a small monthly premium of less than $35. Right that instant, if he is accidentally killed, his family will receive $10,000 in cash, $100 a month for twenty years, and another $10,000 in cash at the end of the twenty-year period, or a total of $44,000. In one hour, the man could create an estate in the event of his accidental death that in the ordinary ways of accumulating interest and principle would require over forty years of making payments. Like carrying the battleship over the mountain, this estate can be created with only a small part of the effort that would be ordinarily required.

An automobile jack is a simple gadget with no power in itself, and yet, if we have automobile trouble, how handy it becomes. It's a very foolish man who starts across the desert without an automobile jack. Likewise, a life insurance policy is a simple financial tool, but when our physical breakdown comes, what a tremendous thing it is.

Similar to what we might call the laws of mechanical and financial advantage is what we might call the law of social advantage. For example, there's a little "jack" that we might carry with us that is called a sense of humor. Think how much less effort it is to jack up our social automobile if we have this tool than if we don't have it. There's a social "block and tackle" that we call a smile. An electric lineman once came in contact with a live wire, and the left side of his face was paralyzed. The jury, in considering the damages, asked him to smile, but he could only smile on one side of his face; they subsequently awarded him $100,000 damages. If half a smile is worth so much and yet it costs nothing at all, then we certainly ought to have it in our "social tool chest" and keep it in good working order, ready for constant use. It's worth a million dollars and yet it doesn't cost a cent. However, we should also remember that one who *doesn't* smile may not be any better off than one who *can't* smile.

There's a social "lever" that we call reputation. What multiplied power and greatly increased strength it gives us if we have earned the right to have people think of us as persons of unquestioned integrity who are fair under all circumstances. regardless of the consequences. A man of genuine character can carry a social battleship over a mountain with strength to spare.

Men have developed extensions to the senses. Through the power of television, we may see across nations; with a telephone receiver, we may hear across continents, though oceans roll and roar between; with a microphone, our voices may be heard around the world; with the wings of jet propulsion, we can travel faster than sound. However, the greatest area for extending ourself is through the use of the social, mental, spiritual, or personality tools that multiply and magnify our strength.

The Master gave us a formula for increasing our strength when he said, "If ye have faith as a grain of mustard seed, ye shall say unto this mountain, Remove hence to yonder place; and it shall remove; and nothing shall be impossible unto you." (Matthew 17:20.)

Prayer and righteousness and dependability also multiply our personal power, and we ought to make a list of these marvelous instruments that come to us without cost so that we may store them in the "toolshed" of our lives and use these powerful laws of advantage.

5 The Law of APPRECIATION

Two sections make up the law of appreciation. One is to be sincerely sympathetic with an understanding of other people; the other is never to count too much on appreciation for ourselves no matter how deserving we may be. We should remember everything that everyone does for us, but we should quickly forget that which we do for them.

One of the strongest hungers in human beings is the desire to be appreciated. Everyone wants to be liked. No one wins the esteem of another quite so quickly as the one who feels and shows appreciation for others. There should be genuine regard for every good thing that the other person is and does. Cicero said that "gratitude is the mother of virtues." Gratitude is also the sign of a noble soul. It always draws out the best in others. It always pays the largest dividends. To give appreciation is one of the best and easiest ways to gain power.

One of the serious weaknesses in human character is the fact that people so often fail to give appreciation to other people as the other people think they should be appreciated. One outstanding example is the lack of appreciation in children. One father can support ten children, but who has ever seen ten children who were able to support one father? If we loan a man money when he is broke, almost always he becomes an enemy and, in addition, he is reluctant to repay the money unless we foreclose his home or hurt him bad enough in some other way. Try it if you don't believe it. Do someone a favor and see what happens.

We know of thousands of cases where an employer has taken a young man into his business or home, taught him his business, financed and helped him, and then, after the young man has learned all the secrets of the business, he becomes the benefactor's most bitter competitor.

Judas was given high position by Jesus, yet Judas betrayed his greatest benefactor for thirty pieces of silver—about $13 in today's currency.

It is, of course, not true that people never show appreciation for the good that is done them. Jesus found ten men stricken with the dreaded disease of leprosy, which had made them unfit for the society of other men. It is difficult to imagine men in a worse situation; yet, after Jesus healed all of them, one of the ten came back to say thank you.

Many would say that one out of ten is a pretty good average. This story is a good one because if one out of twelve betrays us and one out of ten comes around to express appreciation, we are doing as well as did the greatest man who ever lived. In fact, the entire life story of Jesus, including his death, illustrates this fundamental trait in human personality. The greatest benefactor of men who ever lived suffered the most cruel death at the hands of the very people he was trying to benefit. This is not just an isolated case. It is a common weakness in human personality.

Because we are all hungry for recognition, our situation becomes particularly dangerous if we allow ourselves to expect appreciation when the chances are so great that we will not get it. It does not matter why lack of appreciation is so prevalent in human nature. It is enough to know that it is true. Someone has said, "When I do right no one remembers, and when I do wrong no one forgets."

Sometimes persons with a great desire to do good suffer disappointment after disappointment, for not only are they not appreciated, but they actually receive abuse as their pay. Not understanding that this is a common weakness in men sometimes tends to make them bitter and to ruin their lives. They draw into themselves and quit bestowing favors inasmuch as their last attempts were unappreciated or even boomeranged to hurt them.

Withdrawal is the most disastrous course to follow, for the one who withdraws from his fellows is the one who is hurt most. The solution is to eliminate the expectation of praise or appreciation as a motive in our behavior. When we do anything, the criteria to depend on is whether it is right or wrong, not whether or not we expect commendation for it. Then we control the situation in our own minds, and we always receive satisfaction from our good deeds when we have control of the situation. If one out of ten comes to thank us, we are just that much ahead of the game and feel doubly repaid, but if everyone forgets or even turns against us, we will not be disappointed, because we had not counted on it anyway.

The old saying, "Expect nothing and you will never be disappointed," may seem harsh, but it does contain some good logic. We have occasionally seen those people who do everything they do in the hope of receiving praise; and they are always unhappy and disappointed, because in nine cases out of ten, they just do not receive the praise they sought. That is not the way a human being is put together.

A public servant may serve his country faithfully for a lifetime, but because of some little thing, because the wind blows temporarily from another direction, all the good is forgotten. The public is said to be fickle. Everyone has a short memory of other people's virtues or good deeds. It may be too bad, but just remember it is often so.

It is much better philosophy to remember that the greatest person is the one who confers the most benefits, whether anyone remembers or not. We should remember also that it is difficult for others to see with our eyes and understand with our understanding. There will naturally be differences of opinion of our good deeds. It is not likely that one's companions will value him at the same value he sets on himself. We should be prepared for this in advance. We can just as well learn to think kindly of people even when they do not give us credit. It is a practical application of the old story of returning good for evil. This is a great philosophy for happiness, and it is sound to the core. We must learn to serve if we want to progress. We should have the attitude of always doing more than we get paid for. Just think how much good we could do if we didn't care who got the credit.

A good motto to keep in mind is that people who expect gratitude for everything they do really do not deserve gratitude. The history of the world has shown that beneficiaries usually have short memories, and benefactors seldom receive proper appreciation. Moses, like many other great men, suffered most at the hands of his friends. He was the object of continual murmurings by the people he had given his life to serve.

One of the greatest dangers one can place himself in is to take the same attitude toward his benefactors that he does toward his beneficiaries. The law of appreciation says that we should develop great gratitude toward the one and not expect too much from the others. In that way, everyone will be happy, and after all, what difference does it make? We must learn to serve if we want to progress. We should have the attitude of always doing more than we get paid for. Whether we agree with this element in human nature or not is of little importance. All that matters is that we understand and obey the law.

6 The Law of ARRESTED DEVELOPMENT

Our most important responsibility in life is to develop ourselves. This would be a comparatively simple operation if we were made all in one piece. However, we are made up of many parts, including our minds, our wills, our personalities, our instincts, our acquired likes and prejudices—and these are all shot through with the cross-currents of emotions, ambitions, and imaginations.

A human being is a highly complicated machine, composed of thousands of parts, any one of which may get out of order. It is extremely complicated because many of its parts are buried deep in the nervous system or the depths of the subconscious mind, where it is very difficult to make even an inspection, to say nothing of a repair. Also, unlike any other machine, the human mechanism remembers and is influenced by its past.

Less than a century ago the science of psychiatry, which has been called the science of emotions, was born. This was an attempt to x-ray the feelings and personality of human beings in an effort to dig out these unseen ailments, which for all past generations have been responsible for reducing human efficiency to only a very small part of its real capability. The physical machinery of man by itself is tremendously complicated, and when you add to that physical make-up all of the emotions, instincts, mind, and nervous system, he becomes the greatest mystery in existence.

Physicians know that physical sickness and nervous blocks are often the result of emotions beset with mental conflicts. Some of these may have been imbedded in the personality for many years. One of the pioneers in the study of psychiatry and psychoanalysis was Sigmund Freud, who first tried to dissect the mind, as others had done the body. It was he who first talked about the connection between the body symptoms and emotional shocks that had taken place in the early life of a person. As he probed and hunted further into the mental histories of his patients, he discovered many interesting things about personality and the causes of trouble in human beings.

Freud discovered that many people were victims of a destructive condition called arrested development, which has also been referred to as an emotional fixation. There are many reasons why these faculties seem to grow at a greater rate under certain circumstances. As Freud probed into the experience and personality depths of his patients, he found that many of the baffling diseases of adulthood originated in unresolved emotional conflicts of childhood. He found that oftentimes a child had undergone some wrenching experience that had upset his emotional security, and the child was unable to understand or solve his problems. As a consequence, instead of the child's being able to take the experience in his stride and pass it into the normal lifestream to aid him in his growth toward maturity, this inner conflict remained unresolved and was repressed into his unconscious mind. There it imbedded itself and remained out of sight, fixated as some deep emotional force, such as a sense of incompetence, guilt, fear, or an unreasoned desire or prejudice. And from this hidden base, the conflict tended to operate throughout the rest of life, unrecognized by the conscious mind through a source of later emotional disturbance.

Think of the natural stages of growth of a child from the time of his birth. His first consciousness and interest is only for himself. He lives in a tiny world composed merely of himself. Later his world grows to include his crib, the house, the family, then the neighborhood, the school, and the city. What was at first a purely physical world takes on mental, cultural, spiritual, financial, and social dimensions.

At the earlier stages, the only way he knows to get what he wants is to make a nuisance of himself. If he will scream loudly enough, kick his heels, hold his breath, choke, or get red in the face, he can usually frighten the wits out of his parents and make them yield to his wishes. Because this is the only way he knows to solve his problem, it doesn't take him long to become expert in this method of getting results.

In the early part of his life, the child is entirely dependent, lacks vision, knowledge, courage, personality, stability, and is helpless and irresponsible. If a person can get his wants satisfied that way, there is a great temptation for him to maintain those infantile methods throughout life, and he will try to get what he wants in maturity as he did in childhood, by yelling at people or going into tantrums or constantly running to someone else for help.

Adults can continue to be leaners or whiners or cry-babies if they are sufficiently rewarded for those immature qualities. In the formative years of life it is very dangerous to leave our emotional conflicts or any other of life's problems unresolved, undecided, or incomplete. Unresolved problems or half-matured ambitions do not merely disappear when left to themselves; rather, they remain there as festering elements and may later take the form of severe emotional disturbances and prevent one from effectively handling life's problems.

For example, a young boy who was thrown from a horse was badly frightened and hurt. In his immaturity he did not have the judgment to take this experience in stride and master it. If he had been able to get back on the horse to reestablish a proper relationship instead of letting this unfavorable experience become fixed in his mind on an unresolved basis, the event might soon have been forgotten. Instead, he developed a great inner, unreasonable fear of horses and danger that haunted him forever. He never enjoyed being around a horse again. The result was that the unsolved fear embedded itself and in that area he became a victim of arrested development with its distortions in his personality.

This idea of arrested development might not be

particularly important if it only happened once, but when you think of our thousands of fears and dreads, interlaced with a great number of personality and emotional deformities, it is easy to recognize where a great percentage of our problems come from.

Our development in our attitudes toward people is often stopped at a point where we can see, with the mind of a child, only our own little limited world. We have no eye for the welfare of the whole society, and we are intent on hurting those around us who displease us. Under these circumstances we can easily develop, without knowing it, an isolated, fear-driven, hostility-ridden personality, a personality that hangs tenaciously to its immaturity.

Arrested development takes place for other reasons. For example, I know of a young man who went to college and, because of his athletic ability, found himself appreciated for the first time. His particular talents, combined with favorable circumstances, made him a hero in a particular situation, but when he went out into life, his college feats were not recognized. Actually, he found adult competition a little rougher and not nearly as pleasant. He therefore developed some antagonisms to this outside world and tended to crawl back into the memory of his college days and sought to solve his adult problems by the same methods he used in becoming a college hero. His emotional machinery would not let go of his college-boy methods for solving problems. Thus, just as some persons retain their childishness throughout their lives, so this young man tends to remain a college boy.

Everyone should realize as soon as possible that college or the world of business or any other of life's situations is filled with many kinds of people and experiences that are both good and bad, and we must learn to take them in stride and solve them as we go.

We often get in the habit of picking and choosing only those things that suit our fancies, which leads to sidestepping one problem and bluffing past another one. We sometimes avoid things merely because we don't like them, making us grow to be lopsided and misshapen. Then the law of arrested development takes over and does its work.

One may be perfectly matured physically, but in other responses he may be age ten or fifteen or twenty. One man who graduated from college with honors and is the leader of several academic organizations has grown up chronologically, physically, and intellectually, but emotionally he remains a dwarf. Because of lack of insight or of some particularly unfavorable or overly favorable experience, he produces a block or an unreasonable stimulant in his personality so that he gets an unbalanced emotional development; when he is continually confronted by some particularly unfavorable experience, his development is arrested.

In youth, we sometimes tie ourselves to the wrong ideas or people and have a hard time freeing ourselves later on. We should learn to handle each problem and experience as it presents itself until we are able to come to terms with it, until we understand it and are able to take it in stride and resolve it entirely so that it dissolves in our personality instead of growing beyond our control. If we leave the problem unresolved, it imbeds itself and we become fixated at that point of development at which we encountered the problem or emotional shock.

One who aspires to be a great human being ought to avail himself of the research that has been done on personality by psychiatry, psychoanalysis, sociology, psychology, and physiology. If one wishes to give balance and power to his personality, he should learn to understand the problems to which all human beings in their complexities are subjected. He should certainly look out for symptoms of arrested development.

Often we pretend to ourselves that we are obeying the dictates of the mind when in actuality we are obeying the dictates of some unresolved, unconscious emotional or personality force. We continue to seek in infantile ways the solution to a problem that has previously overpowered us, and one of our greatest difficulties is that we do not want to expose this self-deception. Often we do not use reason in connection with our fears and likes. We believe and feel as we want to believe and feel, and as a consequence we develop an unprofitable, unpleasant case of arrested development.

7 The Law of the BOOMERANG

How would you like to possess great personal power? How would you like to be trusted and respected and loved? How would you like to have people always treat you exactly the way you would like to be treated? Here is some good news for you: you can actually have all of those things. The answer as to how you can get them is found where the answers for many of the other important questions of life are found—in the holy scriptures.

Jesus was not just a great teacher—he was also a master of human relations. The greatest statement on public relations that was ever made is known as the Golden Rule, though this title is not found in the scriptures. The Master said, "Therefore all things whatsoever ye would that men should do to you, do ye even so to them." (Matthew 7:12.) This principle has possibilities of both good and bad. Someone has referred to it as the law of the boomerang, meaning that whatever we throw out, we receive in return. A cartoon recently appeared in a newspaper showing two natives from the bush country of Australia. One was saying to the other, "I would like to get me a new boomerang but I can't get rid of this one I already have."

This powerful instrument involving human emotion has also been called the law of retaliation. It involves the ancient philosophy of an eye for an eye and a tooth for a tooth, except the offense is always returned with compound interest. For example, the bombs are getting bigger and the national machines of war are becoming more powerful so that each nation can pay its enemies back with multiplied destruction. In its application to the individual, if we would like to have someone punch us on the nose, we don't need to *talk* to him about it or try to *bribe* him to do it. All we need to do is just give him a good healthy sock on the nose, and we'll be socked in return. We can depend on it. If we want someone to invite us to his house for dinner, we invite him first to our house to dinner and then he will see to it that we get a little better dinner at his house than he got at ours. If we want someone to like us, we must like him. If we want to be trusted, we must trust.

This law represents one of the most powerful combinations of words in the language. In substance it was taught many centuries before it was enunciated by Jesus in Palestine. It was proclaimed by Confucius, Zoroaster, and Mohammed. It has been effectively practiced by many successful statesmen, businessmen, authors, and other human beings. But while this is the greatest statement of public relations that has ever been written, the great bulk of mankind has actually never done very much about using it for their good.

We are like human magnets. Our deeds, our attitudes, and even our thoughts attract in kind. Like begets like. When we know in advance how people will react, great power is placed in our hands, if we have the courage to use it. When we thoroughly understand these laws of action and reaction, then we can stimulate any desired response in other people. If we want smiles, we must give smiles. If we want people to like us, all we have to do is like them. If we speak ill of someone behind his back, he retaliates in kind, only magnified.

If we want to get the best of an enemy, we should be friendly to him. The hottest coals of fire ever heaped on the head of one who has wronged us are the coals of human kindness. To return good for evil is a method of attack that he does not understand; it leaves him baffled and powerless, and we can easily dominate him.

But think what happens when we try to force our way, when we go around with a chip on our shoulder, when we push people around and insist on our rights. We get back evil for evil, gossip for gossip, unfriendliness for unfriendliness, except it is multiplied.

Someone put this idea down in verse; he said:

> Here lies the body of William Jay—
> He died defending his right of way.
> He was right, dead right, as he sped along,
> But he is just as dead as if he'd been wrong.

When we have mastered the simple philosophy contained in the Golden Rule and have learned how to put it into practice, we will have learned much about public relations, salesmanship, teaching, or business success. We will also have mastered ourselves and will have learned how to cultivate self-control.

The Golden Rule is a great way of life. It controls a power that is too strong for anyone to resist. It conquers everything before it. It is a great religious philosophy. If a person can learn how to use it, it can change the whole course of his life in thirty days. It's worth a million dollars, and it is absolutely free.

Try this formula for a few weeks and see what the result is. Above everything else stamp it into your hearts, put it in your bloodstream, and get it into your muscles. Remember the message of this great law: *"Whatsoever ye would that men should do to you, do ye even so to them."*

8 The Law of CHANCE

We have some interesting words in our language that describe events that may exert a great influence over our lives. We sometimes refer to these conditions as chance, circumstance, or luck. The dictionary describes chance as "a happening of events, the way in which things befall."

Great benefits sometimes accrue to those who just happen to be at the right place at the right time, and yet even chance tends to be governed by laws and occasionally can be predicted. We take chances with our marriage and chances with our success. One may just be lucky in meeting the right man or woman, and yet someone has pointed out that success in marriage does not consist merely in *finding* the right person; it is primarily in *being* the right person. And if the marriage partners strictly follow the laws on which marital success depends, such as morality, generosity, fairness, and love, they may largely eliminate the dangers of fickle chance.

A man may have the best chance of eventually owning the business in which he works if he marries the boss's daughter, but the business will reward him according to how he conducts both the business and himself after he has possession.

I recently heard a salesman tell of a very lucky sale he made. He just happened to be on the job at the right time when an important decision was made to buy a large amount of his product. He got another lucky break because the principal who was going to make the decision was a particular friend of his, and he made the sale. Chance and luck can sometimes be very important in anybody's success, but it was probably not chance that had created this friendship or that had gotten him up in the morning and caused him to be circulating where business was likely to be found.

Prospecting is a very important part of salesmanship. Some salesmen are just lucky prospectors; but the more a salesman works at prospecting and the more he studies it and the more he circulates among probable people and the better he conducts his own course, the luckier he becomes.

A man who was being interviewed about his outstanding success was asked, "How did it happen?" He replied that he had always been very successful. Even as a young boy he had usually excelled beyond the point reached by his friends. He said that one of the popular sports of his youth was looking for birds' eggs, and he could always find more than any of the other boys. When asked why, he said he thought it was because he looked in more bushes than any of the rest of them did. Because he looked in more bushes than his competitors, he harnessed the law of probability to work in his interests.

Chance also has certain serious limitations, and if one does not perform his full quota of work, fickle chance may become offended and work against his interests.

Many years ago someone wrote a child's book entitled *The Chance World.* It told of a world in which everything happened by chance. The sun may come up in the morning or it may not, and if it did come up, no one could tell in advance whether it would appear at five o'clock or noon or midnight. In this chance world of fiction, if one planted a field of wheat, it may come up wheat or it may come up barley or it may come up rye or rose bushes or asparagus or apple trees. If one jumped up in the air, he may come down or he may keep on going—and he could not tell in advance which would happen.

Certainly we do not live in a chance world. We live in a world of law and order. When we plant wheat in our fields, the law says that there is no chance that it will come up as barley or lilac bushes or giant redwoods. Seed wheat has been given a basic law with limitations that it cannot overstep, and everyone may discover in advance the laws governing the life and possibility of a kernel of wheat.

The great Creator has established undeviating laws to govern all of the works of his creation. He set our earth in an orbit of 584 million miles, and to complete the trip requires 365 days, 6 hours, 9 minutes, and 9½ seconds. He also ordained wonderful laws governing light, heat, gravity, electricity, and all of the other forces in life. The greatest beneficiary of all of this godly creation is man himself, whom God created in his own image, endowed with his own attributes and potentialities, and gave dominion over the earth and everything upon it. He has made it possible for us to harness the elements and to accomplish miracles in our own interests by understanding these all-important laws. He has ordained the tremendous law of heredity whereby we, the offspring of God, may, by obeying the law, eventually become even as he is. What an exciting challenge that men and women, as the offspring of God, may become like their eternal heavenly parents. How grateful we should be that we do not live in a chance world, and how diligent we should become in following those great laws ordained for our benefit.

9 The Law of COMPENSATION

Everyone seeking success and happiness should maintain an intimate familiarity with the thrilling story of Ben Hur. Over 2000 years ago in the ancient city of Antioch, there was a young Jew by the name of Ben Hur who had been falsely accused of crime and was sentenced to hard labor at the oars of a Roman galley. All day long he was chained to his bench. The galley oars were placed in his hands and a Roman whip was over his head. When his companions were rebellious or revengeful, they brought down upon themselves the lashes of their Roman masters. But Ben Hur was not rebellious, and he asked only that he be alternated from one side of the ship to the other so that his muscles might develop symmetrically.

Ben Hur did far more work than even his captors expected or asked, and every stroke helped to build a more perfect, a more beautiful, and a more powerful body. Not only did he grow physically strong, but his cheerful spirit and fine attitude also built up a winning personality. He won the admiration and friendship of his masters and his own self-respect.

One day there was a devastating shipwreck and Ben Hur was able to save the life of the Roman tribune, and his heroism and excellence won for him his freedom.

Then came the day of the great chariot races. But, as the race was about to begin, it was discovered that one span of horses was without a driver. In desperation the aid of Ben Hur was sought, and the young ex-slave was begged to take the place of the missing driver. As he picked up the reins, a mighty cry went up from the onlookers, for never had they seen such mighty arms or such a powerful body. With great courage and confidence Ben Hur drove the charging horses to a notable victory and won great fame for himself.

There is an old axiom that points out that the Lord always fits the back to the burden. There seems to be a psychological mechanism in each of us that makes sure that every effort we make is compensated for; and frequently, when nature wants to make us great, she gives us some difficulty to strengthen our muscles or some deficiency to promote our resourcefulness.

It seems as though all of our human talents are granted on a kind of lend-lease basis, and they grow best as they are used most. However, when we fail to use them to their limit, we lose their growth correspondingly. Thus, to the exact extent that they are idle, life repossesses them.

A negative manifestation of this law is encountered when one ties his arm up in a sling and sees his muscles disappear. Because the mole didn't use his eyes, nature took away his eyesight. Nature's law of compensation does not merely work in multiplications and additions—it also involves some subtractions. Even Ben Hur had to pay a kind of muscle maintenance charge in order to keep possession.

Ralph Waldo Emerson wrote a great many things about this interesting law of compensation. He pointed out that for every act there is an appropriate compensation. Just as no one can do any good thing without at some time, in some way, receiving a reward, so no one can do an evil thing without suffering a penalty. The cause and effect, the means and the end, the seed and the fruit cannot be separated. The effect already blooms in the cause, and the end always breeds in the means. The fruit is already hidden in the seed.

Emerson teaches the lesson of Ben Hur when he says that if we serve an ungrateful master, we must serve him the more. Build up our balances and put God in our debt, for it is the law that every stroke shall be repaid. The longer the payment is withheld, the better for us, for compound interest on compound interest is the rate of usage under this law. We get paid back in kind multiplied. The negative portion of this law is just as certain: Curses always recoil upon the heads of those who imprecate them. The chickens come home to roost. One cannot do wrong without suffering wrong. And the thief always steals something from himself.

Every time we try to hoard an ability or withhold a service, something is taken from us. As we acquire new arts, we sometimes lose old virtues. As we have built up our means for effortless transportation, many people have lost the full use of their feet. When we support ourselves with various kinds of crutches, our muscles themselves lose their strength. As we depend upon the use of watches, we forget how to tell time by the sun. A notebook may impair our memory. Labor-saving devices make us weak. Those entertainments outside ourselves leavé us bored and eventually incapable of amusing ourselves. In many ways we become weaker by every recruit that we enlist under our banner.

Some men suffer all their lives from the foolish superstition that life is cheating them. However, it is impossible for a man to be cheated by anyone except himself. Some people try to do just as little work as possible and still get by, and that is about all they ever do get. Many people want to be paid before they give the service. They want to receive favors and render none. They want to get out of life all that the traffic will bear. These people are only cheating themselves.

Then there are the Ben Hur kinds of people, those who always try to do more than they get paid for, and then they get paid for more than they do. They try to put more back into life than they take out. These people always go the second mile. They never worry about the pay or who gets the credit. To them it is far more important to think of the good they may do and the service they may perform.

Mr. Emerson says that we should "work every hour, paid or unpaid; see only that you work, and you cannot escape the reward." No matter how often we are defeated, we will succeed if we keep vigorously and enthusiastically trying.

Everyone was born to happiness and victory. No effort is ever wasted or lost. Even the galley slave gets satisfaction out of his work when he performs it on the highest activity level. Of course, we should not be impatient if God doesn't balance the books every Saturday night. To really understand and wholeheartedly believe in this great law of compensation is one of the best stimulants for forming a powerful, winning attitude and bringing about a productive, satisfying success.

It is interesting that God himself is the author of this profitable and exciting law of compensation, and that all of its advantages are pointed toward us. Even the Lord has made himself subject to this law, for he has said: "I, the Lord, am bound when ye do what I say; but when ye do not what I say, ye have no promise." (D&C 82:10.) Again he said: "I command and men obey not; I revoke and they receive not the blessing." (D&C 58:32.)

Recently I attended a meeting of ward officers and teachers. In this particular ward was a Sunday School teacher who had not been as diligent as he might have been in discharging his responsibilities. The bishop had suggested to the Sunday School superintendent that he should sit down with this man and try to establish a basis for a more effective accomplishment, but the Sunday School superintendent had a little different point of view. He said, "If this man worked for me in my business, I would do exactly as you are suggesting. But inasmuch as we don't get paid for what we do in the Church, I think that we should accept whatever contribution this man may feel like making and let it go at that."

However, I would like to voice a little different opinion from the one which says that we don't get paid for what we do in the Church. To begin with, that is just not so. All religious activities are subject to this fundamental universal law, which says that all effort must be paid for and that one can no more do a good thing without at some time in some way receiving a reward than he can do an evil thing without suffering a penalty. This is just not possible.

The great laws of God are all underwritten by his own promises, for he has never given a commandment to which he did not attach a blessing. Through Malachi the Lord said, "Bring ye all the tithes into the storehouse." That is the command. Then he attached the blessing when he said, "And prove me now herewith, saith the Lord of hosts, if I will not open you the windows of heaven, and pour you out a blessing, that there shall not be room enough to receive it." (Malachi 3:10.)

The Lord says that if we obey the law, the blessing will be so great that we will not be able to contain it. From the top of Mount Sinai he said: "Honour thy father and thy mother." That is the command. Then he attached the blessing when he said, ". . . that thy days may be long upon the land which the Lord thy God giveth thee." (Exodus 20:12.)

Isn't it interesting that we can't keep the Sabbath day holy without being paid? Everyone knows that those people who keep the Sabbath day holy will be a different kind of people with a different kind of spiritual credit-balance than those who don't.

All of our blessings come from keeping the commandments. We can't even think a good thought without receiving a reward—it just isn't possible. And we ought to keep in mind that we also can't think an evil thought without suffering a penalty. We can't run an idea through our minds or an emotion through our hearts without changing ourselves. Even God and Satan get paid in their own coin.

God said: "This is my work and my glory—to bring to pass the immortality and eternal life of man." (Moses 1:39.) If he didn't do the work of God, he wouldn't be God. And because we have been given a part in this great enterprise in which God himself is engaged, we must also learn to carry the responsibility. The Lord said to Peter, and He says to all of us, "Feed my sheep." It therefore becomes our work and our glory to bring to pass the immortality and eternal life of man; and just as sure as we fail in the responsibility, we will lose the blessing.

Some time ago I heard a missionary say to one of his contacts, "Missionaries don't get paid. We work for nothing." After the contact had gone I said to the missionary, "That is the most ridiculous statement that I have ever heard. How did you ever get the impression that missionaries don't get paid? I thought the Lord said, 'And if it so be that you should labor all your days in crying repentance unto this people, and bring, save it be one soul unto me, how great shall be your joy with him in the kingdom of my Father!' " (D&C 18:15.)

To dedicated Church workers the Lord says, "Then all that my father hath shall be given unto them." God is a very wealthy person. We all like to inherit from a wealthy parent. And just try to imagine anything more exciting than to inherit from God, to receive everything that he has.

Whenever we do well in that business in which God himself is engaged, we are really in big business in the most stupendous meaning of that term—and that puts the rate of pay of a good church worker up into the highest income brackets. The important thing to remember is that no effort is ever lost.

There is an unerring law of attraction to the effect that, like Ben Hur, each of us will automatically draw to himself the exact reward that he has earned. This was the philosophy of Emerson, and it is also the law of God.

10 The Law of CONCENTRATION

Edison was once asked how he accomplished so much. He said, "It is very simple. You and I each have eighteen hours a day in which we may do something. You spend that eighteen hours doing a number of different unrelated things. I spend it doing just one thing, and some of my work is bound to amount to something."

If you want to be outstanding in any field, there is one important rule to observe: "Concentrate." Get one thing in your mind and heart and bloodstream. Put side blinders on your eyes so you cannot see all the distractions and temptations along the way. Forget the sidelines, and then put all the steam you've got right on the piston head and drive with full power down the main track. Keep out of the mud puddles; stay on the rails. Keep off the detours and sidings and drive straight ahead without continual startings and stoppings. Keep your mind on what you are doing.

When a person concentrates all of his energies in one place, he may hope to succeed. If he divides his time and talent among several enterprises, his chances of success are much less. But should he allow sidelines, chores, hobbies, politics, philanthropy, love of art, and myriads of other distractions to creep into and dominate his waking hours so as to become a passion, his success doom is sealed. It's a different application of the old principle of military success, which says, "Divide and conquer." Armies are weak when they are divided, and so are individuals.

The doctor or lawyer or merchant or prizefighter who specializes is the one who invariably goes places. And yet every day we see persons who cannot resist the lures of the sideshow attractions. They still incline to the thought of cheating this powerful law by having sidelines and outside interests, and by that process they divide their power and subtract greatly from their effectiveness.

Ralph Waldo Emerson wrote two essays on this subject. One is entitled "Power" and the other "Wealth." The main theme in each is concentration. He said, in effect, "Stop all miscellaneous activities. Do away with distractions, other duties, property cares, chores, errands, diverting talents, and flatteries—all are distractions which cause oscillations and make a good poise and a straight course impossible." Distractions always untune us for the main purpose of our lives. Emerson said, "The one prudence in life is concentration; the one evil is dissipation."

As a gardener gets good fruit by severe prunings, thereby forcing the sap into one or two vigorous limbs instead of allowing it to dwindle into a sheath of twigs, so anyone headed for some great accomplishment gets the best results by concentrating his effort in one place.

A child may be perfectly content with his plaything until he sees something that some other child has. The child usually wants everything he sees and drops one thing after another as new attractions are presented. We are very much like children. We want too many things and are not constant and faithful to any one thing. The Bible says, "No man can serve two masters." It doesn't just say that some can't; it says *no* man can. It just can't be done. You can't ride two horses in the same race. The Good Book says, "Keep your eye single." That means to keep just one thing in the focus of your vision. "A double-minded man is unstable in all his ways."

The greatest Christian missionary said, "This one thing I do." That's why he became the greatest Christian missionary. A great Supreme Court Justice, in trying to indicate the value of concentration and how it had helped him achieve such a high place in the legal world, said, "The law is a jealous mistress. It tolerates no competition. The law says to its devotees, 'Thou shalt have no other gods before me.' Success in any field says just about the same thing."

Singleness of purpose and an unwearied will give power greater than dynamite. It's a natural principle. We didn't invent the law and we can't do anything about it, but it is the law. I know a capable lawyer who was complaining about the small income from his law practice. He had inherited some money, and so I asked him how he had invested it. He was very proud of the fact that he earned two or three percent above the regular interest rate; but he had become so interested in how to buy mortgages at a discount that he didn't have time to learn how to be a successful lawyer. He was trying to inflate some investment dollars, and as a result, he had deflated his income until it had almost disappeared.

Or take two doctors of equal possibility. One puts his brains in his business and his money in the bank, while the other tries to play the stock market and care for his scattered investments. He loses his practice while the stock market is going up, and he loses his savings while the stock market is going down. How would you like to have a serious brain operation performed by a doctor who had just lost $10,000 in the market?

Such outside investment cares always detract from success. "Where your treasure is, there will your heart be also." (Matthew 6:21.) This is an irrevocable law, and if we're going to succeed, we'd better have our hearts and our investments and our efforts and our attention in our own business.

We have only so many hours in a day. If we're trying to do four things instead of one, we can do two hours work on each instead of eight hours on one. But we always have to stop when we change directions. This means the loss of the great power of momentum. It also means we've lost the force and power and enthusiasm that comes from concentration.

"Jack of all trades and master of none" describes a human weakness of adults as well as children. We tend to want everything we see. If we take a fire hose and force the water out through the nozzle, we get great power. If we divide it into a spray, it falls softly with no force. The amount of sunlight that falls pleasantly on the back of our hands is just pleasantly warm; but if we concentrate it through a convex lens and focus it into a pinpoint of light, we can develop enough heat to start a forest fire.

It is really surprising how many capable men fail because they "scatter their shot." Some have sidelines. Others let numerous little cares destroy their success. I know of one potentially capable businessman who tends his own vegetable garden, milks a cow, takes care of his yard, does his own landscaping, paints the house when necessary, does the plumbing. He runs the errands, does the shopping, carries his shirts to the laundry, and sometimes washes them himself. When his wife needs to go someplace, he does the baby sitting. Each fall he puts on an apron and helps his wife bottle a winter's supply of fruit. He wipes the dishes and helps care for the children until he probably doesn't know whether he is male or female, businessman or handyman.

This man thinks he is saving money, but actually he is wasting the most valuable thing in the world—the power of concentrated, one-directional, wholehearted effort. He also neutralizes his mind. He thinks like an errand boy and a baby sitter, not like a businessman. His mind is so occupied by this multiplication of little cares that it cannot cope with the important problem of becoming a success. He has even given up the peace and privacy and quiet of his own home by building an apartment in the basement. When the plumbing gets out of order, his renter just calls him; then he takes off his businessman's attitudes and enthusiasms while he becomes a toilet fixer. All of this brings the inevitable result: his wife teaches school to support him.

This is an extreme case, but there are many people who are continually stumbling over a number of little diversions and spoiling their chances to succeed. They are always starting and stopping, always on the detours or sidelines, always trying to save a few dollars or earn a few in competition with the errand boy, the house painter, and the plumber. The bank president doesn't polish the brass or sweep the floor. If he did, he probably wouldn't be bank president very long. A businessman should learn to think like a businessman. His time is too important to compete with errand boys. He should not spoil a magnificent achievement by turning off the fire of his enthusiasm while he fixes the plumbing.

There are some other applications of this great law. Jesus said, "Follow me." He specialized in righteousness and said that he cannot look upon sin with the least degree of allowance. If we are going to follow him, we should follow him all of the time. When we follow the Lord part of the time and Satan the other part, we are doing as much to tear down our characters as we do the build them up. We should think like followers of the Master. When we think this way, we will *be* followers of the Master. We should build up the habits and skills of righteousness. We should allow no exceptions to success. Exceptions untune us and cause destructive conflicts.

The one all-powerful way to bring about godliness and success is concentration.

11 The Law of CONDITIONED RESPONSES

In the early 1900s, a Russian physiologist, Ivan Pavlov, performed an experiment on a dog. For a dog to salivate when meat is brought is perfectly natural, but no one would suppose that a dog would salivate because a bell is rung. Yet Pavlov discovered that by ringing a bell every time meat was brought, he was able to condition a dog's nature so that salivation eventually took place merely by the ringing of the bell without the presence of the meat.

Out of this and succeeding experiments, the great idea of conditioned responses, so tremendously important to every success, entered the thinking of our century. Amazing things can be done to make people different from their natural selves. A man can be made to stop spontaneously when a red light is flashed. He can be made to eat spinach and like it, to kill his fellowmen and feel proud of it, to insult the members of another race and feel justified in his discourtesy. In each case, the result is accomplished by the meat-and-bell process. The eating of spinach by children brings approving smiles from parents; the killing of fellowmen is accompanied by citations, medals, and the cheers of the multitudes; the discourtesies to other races are lauded by solicitude for race purity. In each case, an artificial stimulus is so closely tied up with the satisfaction of a basic need that response to the stimulus is felt as natural.

There are those who feel that we ought to do only those things that we feel like doing; in other words, we should follow the path of least resistance. Under those circumstances, a human personality becomes more or less like a fertile field left to its own devices—a worthless tangle of weeds almost always results.

We are being conditioned every minute by a multitude of forces. Walt Whitman once wrote, "A child went forth each day and became what he saw." Solomon said, "We become what we *think.*" It is certainly true that we become what we *do,* and the wise person is the one who selects his own conditioning agents so that by his own planned conditioning he can tell in advance what the results will be. Think of the innumerable opportunities this gives to a wide-awake occupational enthusiast. We can condition our personalities to where we love every part of our jobs. We can control our thinking, our success, and consequently our personality traits by teaching ourselves to respond as we should.

If Pavlov's dog had been a little more human, he might have discovered that he could learn to salivate (assuming that to be a desirable end) by the mere exercise of his mind. For example, think what happens to your own saliva apparatus when your brain is holding savory thoughts of food in its hungry imagination. I have ridden thousands of miles on airplanes without ever a thought of being airsick, and then one day for some specific reason I had a very bad air experience. For a long time after that bad experience, I used to get airsick almost as I was buying my ticket.

We can learn to condition ourselves for almost any situation. William James announced his famous "as if" principle. This principle states that if one wants a virtue, he should act "as if" he already possesses it, and that particular virtue will be his. Think how important this principle is in all aspects of our lives. By its use we can develop every necessary personal, mental, and spiritual quality as well as acquire all of the attitudes and philosophies required for our own personal successes.

We can condition ourselves to pleasure or unhappiness, to success or failure by bringing the right stimulations to bear in our minds. We use words and pictures and ambitions to condition our responses. Think of the conditioning hatred that was generated in Germany against the Jews by Adolph Hitler in just a few months. Dr. Paul Joseph Goebbels, the German propaganda minister under Hitler, shows himself in his true colors when he said, "A Jew is for me an object of physical disgust. I vomit when I see one. . . . It is a fact. I treasure an ordinary prostitute above a married Jewess."

When we read love stories, think heroism, or practice religion, we change our responses accordingly. This conditioning process goes on with or without our being conscious of it. For example, a certain man was allergic to roses. At the very sight of them he would reveal all the symptoms of hay fever. His eyes would water, his nose would get stopped up, and he would gasp and sneeze. On one occasion, prearranged by the experimenter, this man was suddenly confronted with a bunch of roses. Immediately he had an attack of his hay fever, brought on by the sight of the roses. But these were not real roses; they were tissue paper roses. The hay fever patient and his mucous membranes, sensitive to rose pollen, were stimulated by the mere symbol of roses.

It has never been discovered just how far the mind can go in influencing behavior and welfare. It is certain that it can send one insane or exalt one to unheard-of heights, depending on what he thinks. We can't make a man into an airplane, but we can make him an airplane maker. We cannot make him into an atomic bomb, but we can make him into a creature who feels it necessary to make and use the atomic bomb. Not only can he *be* what he desires, but he can *like* what he becomes. A priest can condition himself to love poverty, a hermit to love loneliness, a pioneer to love hardship, a soldier to love danger.

A great professional man or a great tradesman is one who will condition himself to success. He learns to think success, imagine success, and love success. He also visualizes the many rewards of success. The law of conditioned responses says that we may slant our appetites, our ambitions, even ourselves in any direction to accomplish any given objective.

12 The Law of CONSEQUENCES

In the greatest of all human discourses, the Sermon on the Mount, Jesus said, ". . . seek ye first the kingdom of God, and his righteousness; and all these things shall be added unto you." (Matthew 6:33.)

No one has ever given a better formula for either spiritual or material prosperity. The quickest shortcut to success is to build upon the solid foundation of truth and righteousness. To do otherwise is to violate the very law on which all success is promised. A great verse of modern scripture says, "There is a law, irrevocably decreed in heaven before the foundations of this world, upon which all blessings are predicated—And when we obtain any blessings from God, it is by obedience to that law upon which it is predicated." (D&C 130:20-21.)

One may seek the kingdom of God at the last of his life after having loaded himself down with many sins, but success under these circumstances is much more difficult. We are working against our own interests if we sow the tares first and then hope that by some process the wheat will be able to crowd them out later on. It seems only good judgment to give the wheat a little head start if we can.

In 1922 Gamaliel Bradford wrote a book entitled *Damaged Souls,* eight biographies of near-great men who failed to measure up to their capacities because they had planted too many tares among the wheat. Benedict Arnold was one of these men. In many ways he was thought to be a greater general than George Washington, but he allowed his selfish interests to overcome his sense of right. As a consequence, he is classified by Mr. Bradford and the world as a "damaged soul." The damage to his personality caused by his unrighteousness was responsible for his entire life being marked down in value so that it became of little benefit to him or to his country. This damage didn't injure him just once, but it stayed with him continually, driving away his friends, bringing censure from superiors, and inciting rebellion in his own soul until he finally became a traitor to his country and actually tried to sell West Point to the enemy. The evil first settled in his heart, then ruined his life.

This recalls an interesting custom that a group of ancients had for punishing crime. If one committed murder, for example, his punishment was that he be chained to the corpse of his victim, and wherever he went thereafter he must drag his crime with him—he could not disentangle himself from the result of his evil act. Later, if he should commit a second murder, the load of an additional corpse would be added to his awful burden. Under these circumstances, one would soon discover that it is pretty hard to win the race for success when loaded down with the dead bodies of too many sins. The most disagreeable way to learn this lesson is by actual experience.

This mode of punishment seems severe, but life has a plan of retribution that is very similar to it. In one way, everyone is chained to his crime, for every evil thing we do becomes a part of what we are. If we violate the laws of temperance as given by the Lord, a ruinous thirst attaches itself to drive us farther and farther down the road to despair. Most of us have watched the pitiful struggles of some poor alcoholic trying to free himself from the habit that he has chained to himself. Wherever the sinner goes, as long as he persists in his course, he must drag with him the dead weight of his wrong. It is not unusual for one to wear himself out trying to succeed in direct violation of the laws of success, only to find that he must eventually back up and start over again.

Of course, one of the first principles of material or spiritual success is repentance. Repentance is a wonderful word. It is a wonderful idea. It stands for one of the most praiseworthy actions in life. It signifies a desire for improvement and a turning upward toward things more worthwhile. It is hope and possible forgiveness. It is a new start. But when we build unrighteously and are then compelled to tear down and start over, our time, effort, reputation, and courage are wasted.

There is an old fable to the effect that a horse once ran away from its master, but after a period of time the horse repented and returned and said to his master, "I have come back." The master said, "Yes, you have come back, but the field is unplowed." No matter how sorry one may feel for his days of misspent effort, the work is not accomplished. The prodigal son wasted his substance in riotous living, then came to himself and returned to his father. His father was glad that his son had come back, but the substance could not be recovered; the wasted years could not be recalled; and the thinking habits of the prodigal would probably need a major overhauling.

Shakespeare's Lady Macbeth thrust a dagger into the heart of the sleeping King Duncan while he was a guest in her home. However, she could not get the thoughts of her crime out of her mind, and they finally drove her insane. She washed her hands a thousand times trying to get them clean of the blood of Duncan, but the uncleanness was not on her hands; it was in her mind and heart, where cleansing is more difficult. Hamlet and Macbeth died because the seeds of death were in their characters.

Those striving for success should realize that we are not only punished for our sins, but we are also punished by our sins—and we are not punished once, but many times. We are required to pay for our sins in so many ways: in remorse, suffering, loss of friends, consciousness of degradation, emotional upsets, nervous breakdowns, and, in some cases, as with Lady Macbeth, insanity.

The punishment is always far out of proportion to any possible satisfaction that may be received from the sin. A soldier who betrays his trust for an hour may spend a lifetime in disgrace and humiliation as a consequence. One man spent thirty-four years in the Ohio State Penitentiary for repeated robberies. The most money he had ever obtained at any one time was $60.12, but the habit had entrenched itself and continued to punish him long after his prison sentence was completed.

We suffer for our minor sins as well as our great ones. Jesus said that "every idle word that men shall speak, they shall give an account thereof in the day of judgment." (Matthew 12:36.) Someone has said that we don't need a recording angel to look over our shoulders and make notes of our acts, because what we do and what we think and what we fail to do and what we fail to think become a part of our personalities, and they are written across our lives, in letters of light for everyone to see. All we need to do is turn on the X ray, and we will be recognized for what we are.

The law of punishment known to the ancients is still at work. The punishment of one who tells lies is that he becomes a liar. If a student doesn't study, the sentence imposed upon him is that he must drag his ignorance with him wherever he goes forevermore. The same is true of all our bad habits, unrighteous attitudes, and sinful thoughts. They bury themselves in our personalities like wood ticks, whereupon they become very difficult to deal with.

A roadside advertisement of an oil company displayed this slogan: "A clean engine produces power." That is logical. So does a clean mind and a pure heart. Jesus said, "The kingdom of God is within you." That is where many of the good things are—within us. Jesus said to people, "Fear not," "Have faith," "Be of good cheer," "Be just." He wants men to get the noble qualities of courage, faith, cheerfulness, and justice inside themselves. But inside of us is also where the kingdom of hell is.

We ought to be continually aware of the great law of consequences that says that no wrong ever goes unpunished, and for every evil thing that we do as well as for every righteous thing that we do, there must be a natural and appropriate consequence.

13 The Law of COURAGE

Each of us has two personalities: the personality we were born with and the personality we acquire after birth. It is our "acquired" personality with which we meet our daily problems. Certainly if we had only the personality with which we were born we would never get very far in any area of our lives. One of the most important qualities we can develop in our personalities is courage.

The dictionary says that "courage is that quality of mind which meets danger or opposition with firmness." It may be that we think of courage as being exhibited mostly on the battlefield or in some similarly spectacular place. However, in battle, one is usually fighting for his life; he is functioning under orders and some measure of compulsion, conditions in which it is difficult not to be courageous. But what about our courage when we are alone; when it is just as easy to retreat as it is to go forward; when we know no one will notice us and there will be no condemnation? This is probably the time, more than any other, when real courage is manifest.

We need a great deal of courage to hold us firm against the ordinary pressures of daily life. Just think how much talent is lost to the world for want of enough courage to enforce our daily convictions, or to back up our own planning. Every day sends to their graves obscure men whom timidity prevented from making a first start and who, if they could have been induced to try, might have gone a long way in the race for success. Our greatest fear should not be that our lives will someday come to an end, but rather that they may never have a beginning.

The primary test of courage is in the little things. Single great occasions do not make heroes or cowards; they simply unveil them to the eyes of others. Silently and imperceptibly we grow stronger or weaker until some crisis shows us what we have become. The house built on the sand may be just as secure as the one on the rock if there isn't any storm. It's trouble that reveals strength.

Everyone believes in planning, but how frequently we do not have the courage to follow through and allow some little thing to throw us off the track. When we allow our plans and determinations and enthusiasms to break down, our whole character and personality is adversely affected, and what great value is lost thereby! Shakespeare said:

> The purest treasure mortal times afford . . .
> Is a bold spirit in a loyal breast.

Courage is not easy to develop. We often let go just when we are about to succeed. The great Roman general Cato committed suicide on the very eve of his triumph. Shakespeare tells of England's King John, who lived in the fifteenth century. While he was engaged in a series of bitter wars, the battle had gone against him and he had decided to quit fighting. As he was waiting to surrender, one of his subordinates saw him and said:

> But wherefore do you droop? why look you sad?
> Be great in act, as you have been in thought;
> Let not the world see fear and sad distrust
> Govern the motions of a kingly eye:
> Be stirring as the time; be fire with fire;
> Threaten the threatener, and outface the brow
> Of bragging horror: so shall inferior eyes,
> That borrow their behaviours from the great,
> Grow great by your example and put on
> The dauntless spirit of resolution.
> Away, and glister like the god of war.
>
> —*King John,* Act V, sc. 1

With the new courage and enthusiasm inspired by an inferior, the king put his helmet back on, remounted his horse, and won the battle for England.

It doesn't take much figuring to find out that if we can

develop this quality in sufficient proportion, it will be worth thousands of dollars a year to us in income and much more in righteousness, satisfaction, and peace of mind. How should we go about it? Everyone must solve this problem for himself, but the following suggestions might be helpful.

1. One of the best ways to develop courage is to practice being courageous every day. We can be courageous in little things at first. Courage is made up of a lot of elements, like conviction, enthusiasm, persistence, and a desire to win. If we can use courage in little things, we will soon start winning victories. Someone has said that the morale of an army always breaks down when the victories are spaced too far apart. A successful year is a year filled with successful days. However, if our days are one-half good and one-half bad, we are doing as much to break down the habit of courage as to build it up.

2. We should fill our minds with courage. Read about courage. Think about courage. Admire courage in others. There are stories of heroism and success that will give our minds a positive charge and slant our personalities in the direction of courage. The mind, like the dyer's hand, is colored by what it holds.

3. We are also pushed forward by seeing the opposite quality in other people. Shakespeare said of someone who had lost his courage, "Thy nerves are in their infancy again and have no vigor in them." Cowards are always unattractive, and the life of a coward is a very difficult one that no one wants to imitate. Julius Caesar said, "Cowards die many times before their deaths; the valiant never taste of death but once. Of all the wonders that I yet have heard, it seems to me most strange that men should fear; seeing that death, a necessary end, will come when it will come."

4. We can develop courage by getting an appreciation of the things that life calls on us to do. He is very fortunate whose life's work and religious activities require initiative, resourcefulness, and the ability and courage to stand on his own feet, to do his own thinking, and to carry out his own plans. Any one of us can be successful and courageous until sundown, and if we can do it for one day, we can do it for a week. We can soon develop the stick-to-itiveness and de-

termination to go through with our program to the end of the year, and soon these great qualities begin to stand out in our lives and people will know us for what we have become.

5. We should try to keep all doubts and negative thinking out of our minds. "Our doubts are traitors, and make us lose the good we oft might win, by fearing to attempt." (Shakespeare.) Our fears blind us. It is so easy to quit and to fall by the wayside because we take the easiest course.

We pity the unfortunate people who try to build a successful, winning personality but leave out courage. They often go through life with a fearful, whining, complaining, grumbling attitude of feeling sorry for themselves, without the stamina to stand up and change the situations that may not be to their liking. Everyone is born beneath a signboard that points to courage and says, as did the fiery cross, "By this sign conquer." Courage not only points to success; it leads to pleasantness as well. Every successful life needs challenge. We need hurdles to overcome. We need problems to solve.

A number of years ago, a young man whose great ambition was to learn to be a football player enrolled at the University of Michigan. The coach put the young man to skirmish against the varsity, but he noticed that every time the play came the player's way, he cringed and turned away. The coach finally decided that the player was a coward, and he sent him back to the fourth string and forgot about him. However, in spite of his demotion and humiliation, the young man didn't quit. He had come to Michigan to learn to play football and that's what he was determined to do, whether it killed him or not. So he stayed on the job and did the best he could. The coach began to hear occasionally about the player's determination and mounting courage, and it didn't take long before he was on the first string. History knows this player as Tom Harmon, all-American, probably one of the four greatest football players of all time. He wasn't cowardly; he was just immature.

It takes a little time to develop courage, but it is worth working for. If we succeed today, success will be a little easier tomorrow. We learn by doing.

14 The Law of EGO RECOGNITION

We have been given a natural urge to repeat those experiences which give us pleasure, and nature has provided that the greatest pleasure that ever comes to human beings is the one that comes as a reward of accomplishment. When we go to school, we would rather get A's than D's. When we get married, we would rather be put upon the pedestal than out in the dog house. When we are employed, we would rather be praised and promoted than kicked and fired. This is a natural law of our being, for we all want to be recognized and well spoken of.

Through the desire for approval and accomplishment, nature entices us onward and upward and thereby anticipates and provides for our improvement. This universal desire for reputation and approval excites and strengthens our passion for excellence. It creates helpful rivalry and productive, individual initiative.

This natural tendency to be well thought of has been called the law of ego recognition. The ego is the most important part of a person. It is the seat of consciousness. It is the focal point of all of the satisfactions. It is the center of pleasure, the "self." It is the general manager of our lives. This power is strongest and most constructive when it is activated and used. By this process, nature "bribes" us to do things that are praiseworthy. The most distasteful of life's relations come when people do not approve of us and when we feel that our lives themselves are not worthwhile. On the other hand, nothing is really more delightful than the return of affection and a substantial feeling of esteem.

The ego is with us the day we are born and begins to show itself very early in life. In earliest infancy children cry to get attention. Later they develop all kinds of pranks to show themselves off favorably before others.

Think about how this tendency works throughout our lives for our improvement. We do not wear particular and distinctive clothing merely to keep us warm and dry, but we choose color, style, padding, and whatnot for the purpose of being recognized and approved by other people. Our desires for education, to develop fine manners, culture, influence, power, come largely because of the hunger to be approved of.

Even the accumulation of money is more often than not a manifestation of the ego. Usually people do not work merely to obtain luxury or ease or enough money to supply their needs, because if that were true, they would stop when these things were obtained. But most people work for money long after the actual need has been satisfied, because money in excess of the amount required for the necessities may be used to provide power, prestige, leadership, more attractive homes, late model automobiles, and other status symbols for themselves. These things may also be used to help others, to be able to put ourselves in the right social groups and be approved of by those who, to us, are important.

We should, of course, be careful that we do not allow any distortions of ego recognition to take place. Sometimes when people are unable to get attention through worthy means, they use other means in trying to reach the same end. Criminals try to build up their power and status by theft and crime. Some people become arsonists or gangsters to unlawfully get a feeling of importance and power. Instead of making themselves attractive, some go to the other extreme in dressing in ludicrous clothing, tearing down the establishment, and using other unlawful and improper methods of getting attention.

Our responsibility is to learn to understand the powerful law of ego recognition so that we can use it more effectively. If we can recognize this personality need in other people, we will be far more capable and effective in dealing with them as well as promoting our own interests by being worthy of approval by ourselves and others. But of even greater importance, we can use it in controlling ourselves.

Inertia, that tendency that we all have to "remain at rest," is one of the strongest negative powers in human beings, and we can use the thirst for recognition in ourselves to counteract this damaging influence.

Suppose we make a list of some of the things we might do to develop ourselves in this important success dimension.

1. We should always be very careful of our appearance and grooming, for these are powerful factors in the judgments others form of us. Cleanliness is next to godliness, and our personal and public acceptance is greatly influenced by our physical and moral cleanliness.

2. All of the qualities making for effectiveness, such as planning, industry, study, and our personal relations with people, give that feeling of contentment and satisfaction which feeds this important quality.

3. We ought to make ourselves competitive so we become worthy of our share of the respect and esteem of others. An ambition to excel in worthiness and accomplishment is indispensable to success.

4. We should be constantly alert to our own self-improvement and the service of others.

5. Inasmuch as we all like to be identified with good things, we ought to associate ourselves with worthwhile undertakings, community work, church service, and being helpful to others.

6. Good public and personal relations are vital.

We often make the great mistake of depending upon others for the recognition we crave. Many of life's failures excuse themselves on the grounds that their bosses or their spouses or someone else was not thoughtful enough to give all the pats and praises necessary for their motivation. It is, of course, fortunate when people are considerate and helpful, but why trust something as important as our own esteem to others who more likely than not will forget?

Suppose someone does forget us? Are we going to allow ourselves to be shipwrecks merely because others were not thoughtful? Many really great men, in certain periods of their lives, have been unappreciated. Many great discoverers, inventors, prophets, and social workers have not been given credit for what they have done. Jesus was not patted and praised, but exactly the opposite occurred. Even when praise is not forthcoming, it is silly to go into a tailspin and throw away our chances in life merely because someone was not properly interested in us.

The law of self-preservation requires that *we* provide the substance on which we ourselves will survive. We don't expect someone else to be responsible for providing our food, our health, our muscles, and all the other qualities necessary for our survival. We must develop the abilities and skills to get these things for ourselves. To merely sit back and hope that somebody else will supply them for us is unwise, and we will soon find ourselves in difficulty if we depend upon it.

Why should we not also provide for ourselves the things required by this companion instinct of ego recognition? We know when our conduct is praiseworthy. We can do the things that will give to ourselves satisfaction, peace of mind, and the knowledge of accomplishment far more satisfying than any pat on the back that might come from someone who is not as interested in our success as we ourselves are.

Robert Louis Stevenson said, "I know what pleasure is, for I have done good work." The highest enjoyment is that of being content with ourselves. Meissonier never worried very much about pleasing other people. He said, "I have someone who is more difficult to please than you. I must satisfy myself." And usually, if we really earn our own approval, we will also have the appreciation of others.

15 The Law of ELEGANCE

One of the greatest words in our language is elegance, which is associated with excellence, beauty, and the greatest accomplishment. Elegance is marked by such traits and attitudes as refinement, grace, symmetry, beauty, and good taste. It is the opposite of the low, the commonplace, the cheap, the average. One who aspires to be a great artist, a great singer, a great teacher, an inspiring leader of others, a great orator, or a great poet should have his personality effectively weighted with elegance. Elegance adds luster to the character. It puts a twinkle in the eye, joy in the heart, and glory in the soul. It touches nothing that it does not adorn and beautify. It makes a man manly and a woman delightful and gives charm to everyone.

We ought to be constantly aware of the necessity in our lives of fighting down the commonplace. We should try to rid our speech of slang phrases, to eliminate the coarse and the profane. Cheap habits and unbecoming behavior are not a part of elegance. Some human personalities may drop below the level of elegance to where they resemble a house without lighting or plumbing, interior decorating or outside landscaping. A lack of elegance in speech, thought, dress, or act always makes the body poor.

Our words are reflections from the interior of our minds. It is impossible to hide the deprecating effect on our personalities that comes when we make our person dumping grounds for cheap phrases and shoddy stories. Jesus said:

> There is nothing from without a man, that entering into him can defile him: but the things which come out of him, those are they that defile the man.
>
> For from within, out of the heart of men, proceed evil thoughts, adulteries, fornications, murders, thefts, covetousness, wickedness, deceit, lasciviousness, an evil eye, blasphemy, pride, foolishness:
>
> All these evil things come from within, and defile the man. (Mark 7:15, 21-23.)

The accusers of Peter made another great statement when at the house of Caiaphus they said: "Thy speech betrayeth thee."

In addition to speech, there are many other things that betray us. The habits of chewing gum or picking one's teeth in public are examples of inelegance. They rasp and grate on sensitive nerves. If these personality indelicacies are too prominent they may consign their possessors to lives of groveling serfs both in spirit and in fact. We must not be mean in the things we do nor small in the things we think. What purpose is served by ill-nature or lack of courtesy or permitting slights or getting even or displaying presumed superiority? It is pretty difficult for one to be noble and manly if he is not also thoughtful, clean, and kind.

A quality of elegance cannot be put on and off like a coat. We must be genuine through and through. Certainly we need to definitely establish the practice of keeping our manners well-dressed all of the time. We should be patient all of the time. We should be careful all of the time. We should be considerate all of the time. We should never drift. We should always keep trying to be something a little better than we presently are.

Character ordinarily has the power to win, but it frequently loses when saddled with bad manners and cheap habits, and it is marked down to half-price when its possessor is coarse-grained in his ethical nature, with dirty fingernails, uncombed hair, and offensive attire. Shakespeare said, "The apparel doth proclaim the man." Somebody has argued that clothes don't make us what we are; however, they do make up about 95 percent of all that anyone ever sees of us. And what is even more important, the causes of offensive physical grooming, like spiritual and mental unattractiveness, are among those things mentioned by Jesus that may come out of our hearts to defile us. Excellence and beauty on the inside of our lives will soon manifest themselves on the outside.

We set aside the first day out of each week as a day of rest, a day of inspiration, a day for dressing up in our Sunday clothes to go to the house of worship. It is time for eating our best food and thinking our best thoughts and adding spiritual and mental elegance to our lives. With the proper elegance, we might hope to bring the level of the other days up to that of the Lord's day.

It is interesting that every recorded account of the appearance of God or his messengers upon this earth has indicated his excellence, his glory, and his elegance. As the resurrected Jesus appeared to John the Revelator on the Isle of Patmos, John describes him by saying that he was in the spirit on the Lord's day when he heard a great voice as the voice of a trumpet behind him. He turned to see who had spoken to him, and he said:

> I saw . . . one like unto the Son of man, clothed with a garment down to the foot, and girt about . . . with a golden girdle.
>
> His head and his hairs were white like wool, as white as snow; and his eyes were as a flame of fire;
>
> And his feet like unto fine brass, as if they burned in a furnace; and his voice as the sound of many waters. (Revelation 1:12-15.)

Jesus went into a high mountain and was transfigured before his disciples. The record says that "his face did shine as the sun, and his raiment was white as the light." (Matthew 17:2.) The scripture describes the angel of the resurrection by saying that his countenance was like lightning and his raiment was white as snow. (Matthew 28:3.)

God himself is such a glorious being that no mortal in his present state can endure his presence. A great modern-day revelation says:

> For no man has seen God at any time in the flesh, except quickened by the Spirit of God.
>
> Neither can any natural man abide the presence of God, neither after the carnal mind.

> Ye are not able to abide the presence of God now, neither the ministering of angels; wherefore, continue in patience until ye are perfected. (D&C: 11-13.)

The purpose of our lives is that someday the offspring of God may hope to be like their eternal parents, and the way to be a great soul in heaven is to practice being a great soul here. This means that we should cut out the coarseness, the evil, the low, the unclean. Someone has said that each day everyone ought to think a good thought, do a kind deed, listen to some uplifting music, say a heartfelt prayer, and read an inspiring poem.

Elegance and her twin sister excellence can mold our hearts and make our minds worthy of the greatest success. They also enable us to stand the most rigid inspection at close range. Elegance exalts the mind and makes it magnetic, and nature never allows a truly magnetic personality to long remain unhappy, insecure, or in want.

One of the great losses leading to failure is that we permit damaging leaks to occur, lessening the elegance of our persons. This leakage is caused when we allow ourselves too much of the commonplace or the ordinary or the mediocre in life. We must not neglect elegance either in matter or in manner. Matter is what is said and done, and manner is how it is said or done.

If one ill-feeds a valuable horse, the horse will soon get sick and die. And if one mistreats his personal elegance, something very similar is likely to happen. Our temperament is the total of the emotions that prevail within us, and we can glorify it by fighting down the commonplace and allowing no exception to excellence or elegance. Success is not the power to hypnotize or captivate. Rather, it is the opposite. It is the power to awaken, to thrill, to win, to obtain enthusiastic cooperation from ourselves when our senses have been quickened instead of dulled. Real success does not put to sleep; it awakens and arouses. It does not make us a slave but a brighter, more pleasant, more generous person. William James said, "The greatest use of life is to spend it for something that outlasts it." And life's greatest opportunity is to use our full powers to produce excellence and elegance.

16 The Law of EVIDENCE

In the area of legal procedure, there is a principle called the law of evidence. The object of this law is to get the facts. A judge can more effectively proceed to dispense judgment to all concerned if he has all of the facts upon which a correct decision may be based, but he may play havoc with innocent people if he disregards the law of evidence and arrives at a judgment based in whole or in part on nonfactual information.

In conducting our family affairs, doing our church work, bringing prosperity to our occupations, or making our grand quest for excellence in life itself, we ought to proceed exactly as does a jurist, for our practical problems are about the same. One of the great laws of life is that our judgment is no better than our information.

The three steps in the law of evidence are:

1. Find the facts.
2. Filter the facts.
3. Follow the facts.

A social worker recently said that the reason professional counseling was not many times more effective than it is is that the one seeking help never gives enough actual information about the problem. Many marriages break up because the marriage partners have little factual information about the needs, desires, wants, and ambitions of each other. Frequently a man or his wife will say, "I don't think my spouse loves me." Many people go through their entire lifetimes without knowing the facts relating to this most important problem.

If you ask many people in business or the trades or the professions why they are not making greater occupational progress than they are, often they will be unable to tell you. Many salesmen fail because they don't know the real objections of their prospects. When a buyer is objecting, he may give you a reason that is not really the reason. A good salesman who says, "Would you tell me all of the other reasons you have for not buying," may then discover that the buyer has half a dozen reasons for not making the purchase—and the one mentioned initially may actually be the least important. Likewise, unhappy wives or irresponsible husbands seldom give the real reasons that are causing their marital problems. Sometimes even they themselves may not know what the real reason is.

And so, in addition to knowing the truth, the whole truth, and nothing but the truth, we should also be able to filter the facts and separate those that are important from those that are unimportant. Sometimes we cling jealously to our excuses, our alibis, and our rationalizations, which we substitute for the facts, and for one reason or another we seem to be anxious to keep the facts themselves carefully concealed.

Adolph Hitler is a notorious example of one who did not always have his information carefully classified. On one occasion during a great rage, he is reported to have said, "My mind is made up—don't confuse me with the facts." In a little lighter vein with less serious consequences, the story is told of a vagrant who was brought before the judge, who asked him, "Are you guilty or not guilty?" The vagrant replied, "How can I tell, your honor, until I have heard the evidence?" While this may seem a little far-fetched, frequently we do have little of the evidence giving us the real facts of life even about ourselves.

It is interesting that the moment of birth is an unconscious moment. No one is actually aware that he is being born when the event is taking place, and usually, we don't realize what has happened until quite a long time after it has happened. Sometimes we never really do find out that we have been born. Someone said of his friend, "He doesn't know that he is alive"—and that frequently is close to the truth. It may take us a year or two to find out that we have been born, but in the balance of our lives many of us never discover why we have been born or what we are going to do about it. In filtering the facts we should determine which attitudes, habits, skills, and personality traits are good and which are bad, which will tend to weakness and which to strength, which will make us happy and which will make us unhappy. The only person who can supply us with much of this information is ourselves. If we have the facts and know which are important and which are unimportant, then we will be able to set goals, develop aims, cultivate ambitions, and make decisions. To one who does not know where he is going, no winds are favorable.

Many of the facts of life themselves are not as important as what we think about them. Sometimes we don't actually care about the facts themselves, but base our lives on how we feel or what we hope or what we imagine them to be.

Human relations is one area where it is very necessary that we learn to distinguish between facts, half-facts, and falsehoods. Much of the information we get from newspapers or hear from others is usually only partially true. Some people believe and are guided entirely by what they hear, and the last man they talk with determines their belief. This type of personality can be destructive to the public confidence.

Others may become expert in distorting the facts. For instance, there are some politicians who deliberately try to deceive people. There are also ministers of churches who claim to be representatives of God himself and who pretend to deal in the sacred commodity of truth, but who make all kinds of misleading and false statements, even though the truth is available to anyone. There are some religious leaders who greatly resent their members considering other information, no matter how factual it may be.

Genuine success in every field must be founded on truth and righteousness. Here is an interesting exercise in human research. Select two groups of people in any field, one representing your ideas of failure and the other corresponding to your ideas of success. Then find out what makes the difference. In the process of getting the facts, you may teach yourself a great lesson in cause and effect. Nothing ever just happens. There is always a reason. Usually the man who is successful and whom we admire is the one who sticks to the truth and knows what he is talking about. He does not try to comply with the desires of every person he meets so that he shifts with the wind like the weathercock. The factual man is the man who can't be blown about by every gossip tale that he hears. He doesn't become excited or downcast at every little fear. He has not only formed the habit of separating the wheat from the chaff, but he has also learned to separate the good wheat from the bad.

If one learns how to get the facts and eliminate all else, he will develop the great power that goes with accurate thinking and good judgment. A man of good judgment might be compared to the pile driver who strikes a ten-ton blow, as compared with the man who is careless with his facts and consequently has a tackhammer influence. Few things breed confidence in our friends more quickly than for them to find out that we do not deal in gossip or hearsay.

Not only should we always find the facts and filter the facts, but we should also always follow the facts. Many people do wrong knowingly. Sometimes we follow our desires or our personal interests or our urges instead of what is right. We frequently substitute expediency for facts.

When we are trying to decide whether or not a certain course is proper, if our own interests are involved, we should keep in mind that it is almost impossible to believe a thing that is against our own welfare. It is even more important to learn to think accurately where we ourselves are involved than it is to think straight when we are dealing only with others. Expediency can change our viewpoint very quickly.

The man who has attained a high degree of accurate thinking is able to speak of his enemy without exaggerating his faults or minimizing his virtues. It is much easier to repeat doubtful or inaccurate rumors when they have to do with someone of whom we are not particularly fond. We should train ourselves to follow the facts instead of delusions or prejudices, hatred, envy, or wishful thinking. An accurate thinker must be fair enough to look for virtues as well as faults in situations or in other people, for it is not unreasonable to suppose that all men have some of each of these qualities. It might be a good exercise to spend as much time thinking up excuses for others as we do for ourselves; otherwise we will be deceived.

No one can afford to deceive others, and certainly we cannot afford to deceive ourselves. We should develop an intellect like a clear mirror that sees all things in correct proportion, not distorted as in the mirrors of circus sideshows, where reflections are twisted up into convex or concave planes so that we cannot see the truth of the facts even though we have them directly before us.

Absolute fairness is very important. Whether the facts are for us or against us should make no difference. We should have a sense of objectivity about our own interests and not see them in the distortion of light or gloom.

Someone put this idea down in verse when he said:

I looked at my brother through the microscope of hate,
And I said, "How mean my brother is."
I looked at my brother through the telescope of scorn,
And I said, "How small my brother is."
Then I looked at my brother through the mirror of truth
And said, "How like me my brother is."

One of our greatest purposes in life is to make the best and the most of ourselves, and one of the powerful instruments to help us bring this objective about is our ability to master the law of evidence so that we are experts in finding the facts, filtering the facts, and following the facts.

17 The Law of EXAGGERATION

In many ways the business of life is "funny business" filled with contrasts and various shades of challenge and meaning. Manufacturing can be done on a formula; chemical reactions can be put down on paper; they never change. But to write the directions of human success or any kind of personal achievement is not quite so simple. Sometimes people succeed where we can't explain their success and others fail where the formula says they should have succeeded. The personality factors that determine our success are made up of many parts; each has been included by creation for a helpful purpose, though we may not recognize the functions served by a particular quality.

For example, we have often heard that the trait of exaggeration is undesirable. But a quality that is so prominent in human nature must have been put there for a good purpose. There are areas where the ability to exaggerate is very helpful if its constructive function is understood.

For example, the schoolteacher writes on the blackboard with enlarged letters so that those in the back of the room can see and understand. A scientist looks at bacteria through a powerful microscope that increases the size of the bacteria by a few million times in his eyes. The microscope does not actually make the bacteria larger; it only makes them appear larger so the scientist can work with them more effectively. Astronomers look through telescopes that not only enlarge the planets studied, but obligingly bring them a few million miles closer as well. The planet does not actually come closer; it only seems closer. It is an optical illusion, but it is a very helpful one.

People have developed great convenience and efficiency for themselves by putting bifocal glasses on their eyes. When they look at something close they look through one part of the glass; when they want to see something in the distance they look through another part.

The natural inborn tendency in human beings to exaggerate shows up early in life. If you want an indication of the tendency to exaggerate, put your tongue into the cavity of your tooth. The tongue improperly reports to the brain that the cavity is many times larger than it actually is. Children usually live in a beautiful imaginary world where things are enlarged or contracted by them to suit their convenience, and the parents and homes of the children are given an important magnificence that can lift them up to God. If we look at our own children and compare them with others, it is natural to see our own many times fairer than anyone else's.

Isn't it strange that everyone in the world is great and good and fair in the eyes of some people though they may be extremely small and undesirable in the eyes of others? Wouldn't it be a humdrum life if we saw our own children or our own goals through the same eyes with which we look at our neighbors' children or our neighbors' goals? Charles Dickens once said that everyone should think well of his own business. Everyone ought also to think well of God and his family and himself. That usually involves some enlargements of the ordinary.

Because nature has provided us with the wonderful ability to see things in different lights, according to our interests, the mind becomes all-powerful and, as John Milton observed, "can make a heaven of hell or a hell of heaven." The young wife filled with attitudes of love and ambition can see her struggling husband as Sir Galahad in glistening armor, and he may behold her through the dishwater as a fabled and sabled princess. To reverse this process can create a very hell on earth.

Just think of the thrill and excitement the ability to exaggerate can give to what otherwise might be an ordinary existence. You remember Alfred Lord Tennyson's story of the knight, Sir Launfal. He gave up wealth, comfort, friends, family, and position and spent his life in search of the Holy Grail. He often had nothing to eat and had to sleep on the ground, but always before his eyes was the shining vision of the enlarged object of his quest which led him on with a joyous and happy heart, making his life a thrilling adventure with dreams to harmonize.

The quality of exaggeration with a vivid imagination helps us to paint pictures and dreams to correspond with our hopes. The importance of life is sometimes painted in drab colors and life's music is tuned down to seem ordinary and unexciting. We need the ability to look at the world through rose-colored glasses and give life the importance that it will have when we see it in the light of eternity.

Much of success consists in knowing which things to exaggerate and which to reduce in size. If we look at an object through one end of the telescope it looks very close and very large; if we look through the other end it looks very distant and very small. Our success depends largely on our skill in knowing which end of the telescope to use on any given occasion.

If one would like to be a happily married man, he should look at his wife's virtues through the end of the telescope that magnifies, but always look at her faults through the little end of the telescope. By this process virtues become mountains and faults become molehills.

The story is told of an Arabian sheik who looked at the figs he was having for dinner through a magnifying glass, and the figs seemed to be crawling with all kinds of horrible-looking little bacteria. This spoiled his present and future dinners, because he had no way of knowing that these bad forms of bacteria were placed there in his interest. Many of the problems and disciplines of life are also given for our benefit; sometimes they are most productively utilized by looking at them through the little end of the telescope, and sometimes we need to turn out the vision altogether. On the other hand, we ought to amplify the vision of our faith so we can see across the boundaries of mortality to the future scenes as they will someday appear in reality.

The great scriptures and our inspired imaginations give us a supermortal picturing power wherewith we can enlarge our objectives and make ambitions and pleasures more intense and meaningful. Many people in the most ordinary situations live in the presence of angelic music and colorful visions. This quality enables the most humble person to see his own objectives as well as himself multiplied in importance and destiny and greatly increased in fascination. On the other hand, we see other people in an entirely ordinary light. Very few people have ever indicated a desire to trade circumstances with anybody else. No matter how bad off we may be, it is common for us to see our troubles less and our pleasures more than those of other people.

Some people may think that to deliberately change the size of things we present to our minds and emotions is a form of misrepresentation. Actually it is not, for as Paul says, "For now we see through a glass, darkly" (1 Corinthians 13:13), and our exaggeration helps us to lighten things up and to see them as they will sometime actually be. The microscope of the doctor is a justifiable misrepresentation made for the benefit of everyone. So is the telescope of the astronomer. One of the greatest inventions in the modern world is the anesthetic whereby the amount of pain we are asked to endure is reduced. We have an even greater invention in this direction made by God himself. It is called repentance and reformation. To practice repentance will tremendously reduce the amount of pain we will be asked to endure during our eternal lives.

The Lord has also given us a way by which we may enlarge our eternal success and happiness. The family has been ordained as the basic unit of society and the starting point for most of our love, happiness, and education; and if our family success is increased, our happiness and eternal welfare are greatly magnified. It is not necessary that the intensity of the love of a parent for his child should be shared by others. Therefore, even from an impartial point of view, the parent's feelings for the child are not a misrepresentation, and yet they contribute vastly to the happiness of those participating.

A good cook is one who makes ordinary things extraordinarily delightful. A great artist or sculptor or writer is one who makes ordinary things more constructive and attractive by putting measured, metered, and rhymed words and ideas together interestingly and setting them to music.

The effective, judicious use of the ability to enlarge upon our benefits and reduce our problems is probably the greatest single source of happiness. A little girl said that her grandfather always put on his red glasses when he ate cherries because it made the cherries seem so much bigger and redder than they actually were. If we owned a famous painting, we would certainly hang it where it would get the best possible light to add to its beauty and importance. To always put our best foot forward may also be a very worthwhile form of misrepresentation.

Some unhappy people reverse this process, always with disastrous results. They fight their jobs; they look at their employers through the wrong end of the telescope; they tear down heroes; and when they say "Tell it as it is," they mean to magnify the worst instead of the best. They make molehills out of virtues and mountains out of faults. Some people even look at themselves through the belittling end of the telescope, which produces so much discouragement and despair that life itself seems not to be worthwhile, because virtues appear as molehills and faults become towering mountains.

The dictionary says that to exaggerate is to present extravagantly, to increase immoderately, to heighten unduly, to magnify, to glorify, to increase the force, strength, or intensity of. What a constructive direction that is for making the best and the most of our own lives!

Enthusiasm, cheerfulness, and good attitudes grow out of our satisfactions, and because the tendency to exaggerate was put in our nature for our benefit, we ought to learn how to use it to our best advantage. How inspiring to see a doctor or a teacher or a salesman who has extraordinary love for what he is doing and those whom he serves and who exaggerates in his own mind the importance of his calling. A little of this kind of exaggeration in the right places makes everyone more enthusiastic, more devoted, more capable, more happy.

On the other hand, what great benefits are born when one turns the little end of the telescope on slights, bickerings, and the unpleasant things that are best forgotten as quickly as possible. The man working for success should look at his troubles and obstacles through the little end of the telescope to reduce discouragement.

The freedom to exaggerate is one of the great freedoms, and to know when to reverse the telescope is like painting a great picture; it's a fine art. It is one of the greatest good fortunes of our lives that we may enlarge to our heart's content the importance of those things that are good for us and will bring us eternal life and eternal happiness, and blot out our attention to those things that otherwise would draw us down.

18 The Law of EXAMPLE

On one occasion Thomas Carlyle made a statement about the peers of England that we might use for our own success. We remember that England and the nations of her empire are the only nations that have ever made the idea of democracy and free enterprise work on a large scale over a long period, and Carlyle gave credit to the system of government that obtained in England from the time of the Norman conquest down to the time of Charles I, when England was ruled by peers.

The king appointed peers, or specially selected representatives, to perform for the people of England the function that we are supposed to perform for each other in our businesses, our professions, and our families. Carlyle said, in part:

> Men were appointed peers who deserved to be appointed peers. They were outstanding men, energetic and capable. They were all royal men with minds full of justice and honor and humanity and all kinds of qualities that were good for men to have who ought to rule over others. A peer conducts himself in a solemn, good, pious and manly way. He has hospitable habits and is valiant in his procedures throughout. A king with a noble approximation of what is right had nominated this man, saying, "Come you to me, sir,

> come out of the common level of the people, come here and take this district of country and make it into your own image more or less. Be a king under me and understand that that is your function." I say that this is the most divine thing that a human being can do to another human being and no other thing whatever has so much of the character of God almighty's divine government as this thing we see that went all over England, and that is the grand soul of England's history.

Now in a little different way, it seems to me that that is about what life or the church or our profession says to us. "You come here and take this section of this business or this responsibility in the church or this family or this social situation and make it into your own image, more or less." And isn't that exactly what everybody does? The greatest power in the world is the power of example. We do the things that we see other people do.

Example is how we learn to walk and to talk. It is the process by which we get our manners and our morals and learn to do almost every other thing. The reason that one baby learns to speak English and another learns to speak Japanese is that they have a different kind of example. The reason we dress as we do is because we are following the example of someone else.

If I had seen you eating your breakfast this morning, I would probably have discovered that you ate with a fork held in your right hand. Some time ago in Australia, I discovered that the Australians eat with a fork in the left hand. And if these same people had been born in China, they may not have used a fork at all, but they would have used chopsticks.

And so it is with almost every other activity in life. No one walks alone. Each is standing at the head of some kind of caravan and is largely responsible for those whom he leads.

We have many other illustrations of this powerful law of example. When Alexander the Great was thirteen years old, his father, King Phillip, obtained a Macedonian philosopher, Aristotle, to be Alexander's companion and tutor. Later on, Alexander said that Aristotle was his father. What he meant was that while he had received life from

Phillip, it was Aristotle, his teacher, who had taught him how to live. Later Alexander said that he was more indebted to Aristotle for knowledge than he was to Phillip for life, and when he referred to Aristotle as his father, he implied that while he had received his body from Phillip, Aristotle was the father of his mind.

We have no choice in the selection of our physical parents, but we may choose our own mental, spiritual, and moral progenitors from among the greatest people on the earth. There is always great power in fine ideas when they are reinforced by an inspiring example. Zeno bid the Greeks to imitate Pericles, and while this may seem like counterfeiting to those who would not understand, yet even this process, if religiously followed, might in time instill into them a real love and knowledge of those noble qualities for which the famous Athenian was so noted.

Physicians form diagnoses by comparing healthy and diseased bodies. We develop success by comparing healthy and diseased personalities—Plutarch, the great Greek moralist and biographer, spent his years writing about the lives of men, good and bad. He said:

> It was for the sake of others that I first commenced writing biographies, but I find myself proceeding and devoting myself to this study for my own sake. The virtues of these great men serve as a sort of looking glass into which I may see how to adjust and adorn my own life. I am thus enabled to receive and retain images of the best and worthiest characters and also to free myself from any ignoble, base, or vicious traits.

Plutarch once wrote a provocative discourse about the advantages we can derive from our enemies, and it was asserted by Cato that wise men profit more from fools than fools profit from wise men, for wise men try to avoid the faults of fools, but not so many fools ever try to imitate the good example of wise men.

William Shakespeare was one of the greatest writers and also one of the greatest salesmen who ever lived. He wrote thirty-seven plays, and out of his brain he created a thousand characters and endowed each one with attitudes and personality traits of surpassing value. Shakespeare saw the various elements of human nature with great clarity. He understood the roles that personality and character play in success. He knew the laws underlying accomplishment and failure about as well as anyone of whom we have record.

Every seeker after success would do well to study Shakespeare and see this interplay of personality traits through the crosscurrents of reason, emotion, and other areas of human nature. Each one of Shakespeare's characters is the personification of some personality trait from which we may profit. We learn courage from one, logic from another. A sense of humor, humility, and all of the other major and minor virtues are exposed to our full view, and they are made easily available for our adoption; the negative traits are also put on display for our inspection so that we may know of their dangers. Then from the whole, we may compare and adopt as we choose.

Greek artist Apelles, who lived in the fourth century B.C., painted his famous picture of the goddess of beauty by selecting the finest features from each of the most beautiful women of Athens, to make his artistic composite of that painting whose beauty and majesty enthralled the world. In the all-important matter of the development of our own personality, we learn fastest by borrowing the ready-made virtues and eliminating the proven vices as we see them outlined in those whom we study, for only as we see them in actual operation and know of their consequences can we understand their values and disadvantages to us.

The ancient Spartans had many good ideas. They understood the power of contrast. Occasionally they would have some of their young men drink large quantities of wine at their public educational festivities so that other young people might see and understand the meaning and consequences of drunkenness. Then by this process of comparison, they could determine whether or not they wished to include drunkenness as a part of their own lives.

When we observe a trait of personality in someone else that pleases us, we ought to try to adapt it for our own use. Think what an upsurge it would give us if we could see ourselves building a more pleasant personality, piece by piece, just as we would build up some other important inventory. A smile is much more becoming than a new necktie.

Honesty has greater usefulness than a new automobile, and a great ability has larger earning power than our rented real estate.

Homer portrayed the great Greek hero Achilles exulting with joy at the sight of his new armor and sword, and pictured him afire with enthusiasm in his eagerness to use them for the benefit of his country. If we could indicate this same enthusiasm to acquire and use new personality qualities and accomplishment skills, we would not long be properly classified as a race of scrubs.

Marcus Aurelius, one of the great emperors of ancient Rome, said that those who worship reason and fairness and strive to develop themselves may make such an improvement that "within ten days thou wilt seem a god to those to whom now thou art only ordinary." He said, "Do not act as if thou art going to live a thousand years. Death hangs constantly over thee. Therefore, while thou livest and while there is power in thee, be good."

The great example of Plato was Socrates, and all his life he quoted and talked about his great teacher. It is said that the words of Socrates used to throw Plato into transports of ecstasies, getting into his blood like strong wine, intoxicating him to a sort of frenzy. Such is the power of a great example, and by the power of great example, Plato fashioned himself in the image of the best that was in Socrates.

There is no better means to progress than to thoroughly understand that almost everything we are, good and bad, we get from others. The law of example is the greatest single determiner of character. Plutarch observed that even horses ran brisker when harnessed to a chariot than when driven singly, because when they were matched one against the other, emulation kindled and inflamed their courage and gave them extra strength. Brave men also provoke each other to noble acts and are strongest when they are united together. Plutarch determined to study and learn from men both good and bad. He said, "I give particular attention to the marks and indications of the souls of men while I endeavor by these to portray their lives." If that was a good idea for Plutarch, it is a good idea for us.

All around us are great people who have been successful in every field. Why not study them more and learn from them what makes them different from us? Jesus told of some great exemplars and then said, "Go thou and do likewise." By this process we may fashion ourselves in their likeness. We have available to us the written biographies of the greatest men, the finest literature, the most inspiring scriptures, and the greatest prophets. The Son of God himself said, "Follow me." He nominated himself to be our example. We can follow him in his faith and in his industry and in his righteousness, and by the power of his reflection we can become as he is.

19 The Law of EXPERIENCE

Suppose that a person endowed with all of the potential faculties of reason, good judgment, and reflection should be brought suddenly into the world completely without experience and is asked to make his own way by himself. We can easily imagine the difficulty of his situation no matter what his capabilities are. To live successfully by oneself would be impossible.

For example, how could one know by mere reason that ice is the result of freezing water, and that glass, which might look exactly like the ice, is the result of heating sand? Or who would be able to know without experience that bread is proper nourishment for a man or a dog but not for a horse or a lion? Who could tell that if a little spark of fire should escape from the fireplace it could eat up an entire house and leave very little by way of remains? Or suppose someone asked you to carefully define and explain the passions of love and hate, or to explain how a human being would behave under the pressure of great fear. No one would be able to understand these feelings unless he had actual experience with them. Thus we see that much of life must be interpreted, judged, and guided by reason based on experience.

When a child feels the sensation of pain by touching the flame of a candle, he learns more quickly than in any other way to be careful in the future not to put his hand in the fire. In building our success in our occupations and in life we should start with the premise that we ought to get a lot of the best experience under the right kind of supervision as quickly as possible.

Fortunately we need not have all of the experiences personally. We can learn a great deal from the experiences of others. The laws governing success and failure are about the same in their application to each of us. Books of science, business, the professions, and religion are filled with the experiences of countless people who have lived before us. They have learned the most valuable truths and made the most serious errors, many of which have been written down for our enrichment and practical benefit, and in every case we are free to accept the good and reject the bad.

We should give a great deal of thought and study to the techniques and methods for getting the maximum good and the minimum evil from each experience.

We can get more out of our experience if we understand some important aspects of human behavior.

1. One of these is classified as the instincts. Nature has equipped us with some powerful natural urges or tendencies. We have a natural instinct for self-preservation; in the days of Job it was said, ". . . All that a man hath will he give for his life." (Job 2:4.) We have a powerful sex instinct to acquire a family; this was intended for the preservation and multiplication of the race. We have a competitive instinct; every person is endowed with a natural desire to compete and excel.

We have a moral instinct; God has given everyone a conscience with the power and the ability to know good from evil. We have an acquisitive instinct—we like to own property and feel secure. We also have an inquisitive instinct, for we are all naturally curious. From our earliest beginnings, we want to know things and go places and have new and interesting experiences; this is the foundation of our education and growth. Everyone has a kind of God instinct, an upward reach, a desire for improvement, to become better than we presently are.

We have a lot of other interesting inborn qualities that we should understand, and we will progress much faster by arousing and developing these instincts in ourselves in such a way as to give them their greatest strength.

2. The second aspect of human behavior is to have definite programs for eliminating our weaknesses. Good and evil cannot successfully coexist. During the Civil War Abraham Lincoln said that no nation could exist half slave and half free, and it is difficult to reach success when our lives are half good and half bad. One of the early steps that anyone should take in any undertaking is to make a list of those things that he just must not do under any circumstances. Man has some natural vulnerable points. There are certain places where we tend to habitually fall down. We live in a world of contrasts, the most important of which is good and bad. At the head of good is God, while the chief sponsor of bad is Satan. The weakness that has taken the greatest toll is our natural tendency to evil. Many civilizations have been destroyed and much individual success has been lost because of sin. People become angry, they get lazy, they transgress the law, and trouble always results.

3. When we understand these natural tendencies implanted in our souls by creation itself, and when we have gained a clear understanding of those things that we must not do, then our time is free to spend in doing those things that we should do. From the very beginning men and women have been engaged in the great struggle for success. The reasons why so many fail have been recorded to let us know which areas should be avoided. Literature has recorded the successful experiences of great human beings for our benefit. It is perfectly clear to us why such men as George Washington and Abraham Lincoln and Thomas A. Edison and Henry Ford and Albert Einstein have been successful. Experience of people through the ages as well as our great modern-day knowledge explosion gives us a solid foundation on which to launch our own careers. God himself has given us scriptures with all of the fundamental concepts of right and wrong, industry and sloth, excellence and failure, and if one is alert and will follow instructions, no one need get off that strait and narrow path which leads to success. The Son of God himself came here to the earth and established his church and gave us the doctrines of salvation and success. He himself became our exemplar when he said, "Follow me."

What a tremendous addition we can make in our success experience if we vigorously practice every one of his laws!

4. Another fantastic power is called imagination, whereby we can take the individual elements of the success of others and put them together in new combinations. Imagination is a great picturing power. It gives us the constructive ability for invention and development. Life is the greatest and most exciting of all experiences. We are permitted to come into a world that we know nothing about, among strangers, and have the most thrilling, profitable experiences that will not only lead to success in this life but which will also lay the foundation for our eternal success and happiness.

5. What a tremendous privilege we have when we have the absolute freedom to make the best and most of our own lives. We are not placed upon the earth to fill our lives up with experiences of sin and failure. Some time ago I heard a young man discussing a particular occupation in which he had some interest. One of the things he wanted to know was what percentage of those who entered this particular job stayed with it and how many dropped out along the way. The expert whom he was consulting said, "I would like to give you two answers to that question. The first answer is that there is a tremendous percentage who fail. The second answer is that of those who follow instructions, there is almost no possibility of failure."

That might be a pretty good application to make to life. Jesus said, "Enter ye in at the strait gate: for wide is the gate, and broad is the way, that leadeth to destruction, and many there be that go in thereat: Because strait is the gate, and narrow is the way, which leadeth to life. . . ." (Matthew 7:13-14.)

Suppose we tried to picture all of the people in the world and get the percentage of those who have gone down the broad road and become dropouts from material success. We might count those in the crime wave started by Cain and those who were removed from life by the universal flood of Noah's day. We might count those responsible for the destruction of Babylon, Assyria, Tyre and Sidon, Sodom and Gomorrah, Greece, and Rome. We could add those who crucified the Son of God and brought the dark ages upon the world. Then picture those of our own day who cause upheavals among nations, crime waves, divorce and family dissension, and scandals in government, and we might gain a little deeper appreciation of that "strait and narrow way" which leads to success and eternal happiness. Each one of us who has a strong enough desire may be among that select few. We can do this by making every experience a great experience, with no exceptions allowed for weakness, sloth, sin, or failure.

20 The Law of FEAR

A theory is held by some people that fear is a great curse sent to punish those who live upon this earth. While nothing could be farther from the truth, yet those who adopt this philosophy are injured by it. Actually, the ability to fear was put into our personalities to strengthen our courage, protect us from harm, and increase our godliness and our capability for accomplishment.

As a consequence of this misunderstanding about the purpose of fear, many people try, to their own detriment, to avoid or distort or sidestep this important and constructive emotion and the natural fruits that would otherwise come from it. We ought to thoroughly understand the fact that far from being man's enemy, fear is a great and constructive force for good if one is afraid of the right things at the right time. The ancient Greeks even erected a temple so they might show proper reverence to the god of fear.

Fear is the beginning of wisdom, the father of prudence, caution, and foresight. It is a stimulant that keeps us on our feet and moving. A child stays away from fire because of fear; men are encouraged to obey the law because of fear; a young person goes to school and works and prepares himself in life because he fears the results of ignorance and unemployment. We control our conduct because we fear a bad reputation. We work and save because we fear want. We plan and think because we fear the result of a misdirected course. So it naturally follows that we should stimulate rather than try to destroy our fears.

Fear is the warning flag that prompts us to stop, look, and listen. It makes us sharp and aggressive and keeps us on our toes. It puts us on our mettle. The world would indeed be a chaotic place without the great and valuable controlling emotion of fear. The squirrel would not store up his acorns if he were not afraid of the winter's cold and hunger. The lawyer would not prepare his court presentation so meticulously if he were not afraid of failure and defeat.

The people in Egypt built granaries and stored up their corn in the good years so that they could provide for themselves during the poor years—and that is a good program for our present day. The apostle Paul was agitating this fear of want when he said, "But if any provide not for his own, and specially for those of his own house, he hath denied the faith, and is worse than an infidel." (1 Timothy 5:8.) This fear for our family's welfare is a part of that emotion which Shakespeare describes as "the fear that reason leads."

Fears of failure and weakness and consequence also tend to make a nation great and strong and safe. Sometimes in times of peace and ease, a potentially powerful nation may be idle and tend to become fat, lazy, and listless. We might recall when the enemy attacked Pearl Harbor and how America immediately sprang to its feet like a giant. Its muscles became taut; its attention came into focus; its brain became alert; its creative genius began to produce unheard-of inventions and unbelievable miracles of production, all because it was angry and afraid.

Fear pours into the blood a powerful element that multiplies our strength. If our house catches fire, in our excitement we may be able to carry the piano outdoors to save it from the flames, but after the fear has subsided, it would take four people to carry it back in. We can run faster or fight harder or do more work or be more faithful when we are afraid.

Certainly we ought to be afraid of bigotry and pettiness and dishonesty. Fear is also nature's method of individual protection to keep us all safe, honest, and prosperous with a feeling of security for our eternal lives.

It is very important that we understand the purpose and use of the law of fear. Like any other strong, powerful instinct, it can be abused, distorted, or destroyed. For example, when the sex instinct is not controlled, great damage results. When we accept the new morality and say, "Everybody's doing it," and try to convince each other that God has changed his mind or is asleep, our senses become deadened and our fear is reduced to the point that evil indulgence does not seem so bad. If we are wise, we will keep our protective fears alert and active.

James A. Garfield said, "I am afraid to do any evil thing." This seems to correspond with the wisdom of Solomon, who, in Ecclesiastes, gave us a punch-line conclusion when he said, "Fear God, and keep his commandments: for this is the whole duty of man." (Ecclesiastes 12:13.) To fear God and keep his commandments is just not a part of the duty of man, it is not just the most important part of the duty of man, it is the *whole* duty of man.

The meaning of fear as it is used by Solomon also includes a belief in God, a reverence for his judgment, a confidence in his wisdom, and a knowledge of his law that everyone who does wrong must pay an awful penalty and everyone who does right will receive a magnificent blessing, both of which go far beyond the importance of the action itself. On one occasion Admiral Farragut was asked, "Are you prepared for defeat?" The great admiral said, "Certainly not, I am prepared for victory." When we love God, have confidence in his righteousness, and fear to break his holy laws, we prepare ourselves for the most magnificent success.

There are many kinds of fear, just as there are many kinds of courage or industry or faith. There is the fear of the lazy man who fails to attempt. There is the fear of the coward, who wrings his hands and wails his woes but will do nothing about them. There is the fear of ignorance, in which we don't know the difference between right and wrong. There is the fear of the weakling, who is afraid to try. The slothful servant said, "I was afraid, and went and hid my talent in the earth." To him the Master said, "Thou wicked and slothful servant." And then he said to those who were with him, "Take therefore the talent from him, and give it unto him which hath ten talents. . . . And cast ye the unprofitable servant into outer darkness: there shall be weeping and gnashing of teeth."

Fear as an element in education cannot be ignored. It is like a fire; it is a good slave but a poor master. Fear is like strychnine—a great stimulant, but if you take an overdose of either strychnine or fear, it usually signals the end. Let fear get out of control to a point where it becomes panic or hysteria and it causes great destruction.

Many people are always predicting unreasonable calamities, tending to stampede their own reason and the reason of other people. The road to duty and success is hampered by one's fears. Unreasonable fears make one blind and deaf and sometimes dumb, but if it is understood and controlled, fear can become our greatest ally. Shakespeare said, "To fear the worst, oft cures the worst."

The things we fear are the things we are most likely to do something about. It is the comfortable, warm, soft, friendly vices that do us the damage. It is the most pleasant things to which we pay court that eventually destroy us. Usually we are not in danger from our enemies; we suffer more from our friends who praise and flatter us. God himself has said that a man's foes shall be those of his own household. Isn't it interesting that they pick up most of their vices of intemperance, nicotine addiction, immorality, and atheism from their best friends. However, each man's greatest danger comes from within his own soul, which may cause him to destroy himself. A proper fear can help protect us from ourselves.

Everyone who is a candidate for a successful, happy life ought to catalog his fears and make a list of the things that he is or should be afraid of. Then he can analyze them and make plans as to how he can most effectively handle them. The Lord himself has given us one of the best answers when he said, ". . . if ye are prepared ye shall not fear." (D&C 38:30.) What a great statement that is! Individual fears are nature's warning signals to us that in those areas in which we fear, we are not adequately prepared. They are like a red flag, the clanging of the danger signal, an eternal alarm bell.

Motivated by a substantial, well-controlled, well-understood fear, our spiritual and mental muscles can become strong. If we learn how to properly handle our fears, we become courageous, industrious, and productive.

We should not fear fear, but should recognize it and welcome it as an ally, sent to give us judgment and muscle and protection. In fact, the only place where it is possible to develop courage is in the presence of fear. Fear is the moving cause of most accomplishment. We should try not to avoid it, but rather to develop it, for if we would eliminate the cause, we must also do without the result. If fear is removed from the young man, it may mean the security will be taken away from the old man. We should only learn to recognize, appreciate, and control it.

It is a perversion of our personalities to let fear inspire timidity, paralysis, dread, dismay, hysteria, or panic. Shakespeare gave us one of our greatest philosophies when he said, "Cowards die a thousand times before their death; the brave man never tastes of death but once." He said, "Of all the wonders that I yet have seen, it seems to me most strange that man should fear, seeing that death, a necessary end, will come when it will come." We may not always be able to change the time of our death, but we can always be better prepared for it. After all, most of the things we fear are corrected before they happen. The most difficult memory test is to try to even remember the things we worried about ten years ago.

Of all our troubles great and small;
The greatest are those
That never happen at all.

And so we might say to ourselves, "Let not fear prevail above thy will." (Apollo.)

21 The Law of FINANCIAL RESPECTABILITY

Many otherwise good men allow success to elude them because they lack financial respectability. It is not uncommon to see men who are well developed in other parts of their personalities but who lack good financial sense. In human relations, few qualities make one so vulnerable to defeat as the quality of not knowing how to handle oneself financially. One may be weak in some parts of his personality without interfering with his success in other areas, but one who is financially insecure has a difficult time in most other areas of his life. Someone said, "I am not sure just what the unpardonable sin is, but I believe it is the disposition to postpone and evade the payment of one's bills."

Probably few things could be more helpful in developing our religion, our morality, our citizenship, and our own morale than sound financial maturity. A book has been written entitled *How Old Am I Financially?* If we can answer this question, we can foretell much of our own future. It is suggested that each human being should review his financial habits so that they will not hold him back without his knowing it. Here are some suggestions to help us do this.

1. *Develop the habit of paying promptly for what you get.*

There are, of course, cases when installment payments may be all right, but some people want to give us credit when we don't need it, and everyone is suspicious of a person when he is broke. One man we know was otherwise a good member of the Church, but he had the bad habit of asking far too many people to sell him things on a credit that was pretty shaky and then paying for them a few dollars a month. There are few better ways than this to advertise poverty and lower one's self-esteem and public relations.

Through the process of unbusiness-like conduct, creditors sometimes wear themselves out with waiting and promises. What kind of impression does that make? Just think of the person who borrows money and then makes the lender come back again and again, begging and coaxing to get what belongs to him, and then pays it in little hand-outs over an extended period.

If a person needs more money, there is one right good way to get it, and that is to do more and better work. If we always practice spending less than we earn, we will usually have a surplus. But no matter to whom we owe money, we should always be sure payment is made promptly before it is due, or if we cannot make payment, we are the ones who should do the worrying about it. A borrower can make a fine name for himself by going out of his way to let his creditors know that he is on the job and working in their interests.

2. Shakespeare gave some excellent advice when he said:

> Neither a borrower, nor a lender be,
> For loan oft loses both itself and friend,
> And borrowing dulls the edge of husbandry.

It is dangerous to borrow money from friends or associates. Some people spend more time trying to "work their friends" for loans than it would take to earn the needed money; and, of course, people who borrow from or loan to their friends put their friendship in great jeopardy.

3. *Develop financial integrity.*

Some people who are otherwise considered honest develop sneaky little financial habits. They try to "chisel" on a deal after it has been made. They "welch" on their word. They promise but when the time arrives, they put us off. They seem to completely disregard our pleasure and convenience. They have a lot of excuses, but they don't pay. They like to eat if someone else will pay the check. An attitude of trying to get something for nothing is very bad business and usually backfires with disastrous results.

4. *Build a financial reserve.*

No one would think of starting to drive across the desert in his automobile without a spare tire. No one would feel entirely safe on a dangerous ocean voyage without a lifeboat. Just so, every human being ought to have a substantial financial life preserver in the form of a sizeable reserve. Having money in the bank gives a person a spirit of self-confidence. It builds determination, self-reliance, self-respect, self-control. A reserve is one of the best weapons for the conquest of fear.

5. *Have adequate life insurance protection.*

Every man who gets married and brings children into the world should have an adequate life insurance program to provide them with financial responsibility in the event of his death.

6. *Use personal credit wisely.*

In everyone's life there sometimes come emergencies when he needs extra money. Some people solve this problem by (a) letting their bills go, thus inconveniencing those with whom they do business; or (b) borrowing little dabs of others' money on a friendship basis from personal acquaintances.

Both of these methods tear down one's public relations and peace of mind. A person of sound financial sense will establish his credit so he is prepared for emergencies long before they happen. The financial institutions with which he has done business in the past should have absolute confidence in his ability to earn, his integrity in meeting his obligations promptly, and his absolute honesty. He never tries to cut corners. He never disappoints anyone. He is never late and never makes his creditors remind him that the payment is overdue.

7. *Develop a sense of community responsibility.*

A part of everyone's financial education should be the recognition of his responsibility to the community in which he lives, not just by paying his taxes—in that he has no choice—nor in just doing his part of church and community work. The person who feels that the world owes him a living always has an unhappy time trying to collect it. However, the one who feels that the welfare of the community is his responsibility will get his contribution back increased manyfold. Part of all one earns should be put back into the community, just as a good farmer reserves his best grain to seed the soil out of which his profits come.

8. *Establish financial respectability at home.*

An easy place to take one's own financial measure is to check up on how one handles himself financially in his own home. Some men compel their wives to beg and bribe and crawl and plead for money. Others give them a definite allowance each month. Some of the advantages to this latter procedure may be as follows:

a. The wife becomes the financial manager in the home. She pays the bills, looks after the details, oversees the shopping, and leaves the husband's time free for one of his major responsibilities, which is to earn the money.

b. She is thereby trained in handling money, which is of great value to her now and in the future. She learns to stand alone on her own financial feet, which may be of great value should future circumstances make that necessary. Some men fail in this area because their minds are cluttered up with a thousand little distractions and side issues that could be much more efficiently handled by the wife.

c. She develops more interest in the business and economy of the home as well as in the business from which the income is received when she is an interested partner rather than when someone else makes all of the financial decisions.

d. She has a definite income so that she can make plans and use her intelligence for the welfare of the unit.

Now, suppose there isn't always enough money to go around. No one always has an income and an outgo that exactly fit each other every month. Emergencies sometimes throw a large, unlooked-for expense into the debit side of the monthly budget. How a man handles his wife financially may indicate how he handles other people. It's pretty hard to be one thing in one's own home and something else elsewhere.

I know a man who thinks of himself as "giving" his wife something when he merely turns over to her the money to pay the bills. And if on the first of the month he hasn't enough money to go around, he merely tells her she'll just have to wait a week. Then if in a week the money is still not forthcoming, he'll put her off again. Sometimes he may get three or four months behind. His wife is embarrassed before all of the people with whom she does business. She can never make her plans in advance, because her husband is financially undependable. Not only do the family relations deteriorate with the outside people with whom business is done, but internal relations begin to crumble as well.

Now think of another man who sends his check to the bank and the bank automatically deposits the agreed-upon amount in the wife's account. He is the breadwinner and he bears the load that goes with that responsibility. Why should a person be more dependable with his creditors than he is with his own family? Irregular times will come, and so he should prepare for them in advance. Home is a good place to practice these major virtues. A wife above all other people should know that her husband can be absolutely depended upon and that her share of the money will be in the bank not later than a couple of days before it is due.

Many divorces and hard feelings between husband and wife are concerned with finances, and not always with the amount. Often trouble arises because dependability and understanding of having everything satisfactorily have not been worked out in advance. If people plan their affairs and then learn to be financially responsible, they seldom have to discuss finances. Few things build up good internal relations like financial understanding, confidence, and respectability. If you want peace of mind in your work, get financially organized at home.

There are some people who write checks that are not covered by sufficient funds. In public relations this is close to suicide. It is also legal suicide in some cases. Everyone should learn to be a good financial planner. He should know how much money he needs and the amount of work necessary in order to produce it, and a little bit extra. Some people will go to almost any limit to keep from real, honest-to-goodness, productive work. They will lie down on the job, shirk responsibilities, dodge their creditors, jump their bills, borrow money from their friends, or even beg from their children. And then much of this is wasted on tobacco, liquor, gambling, and other sinful vices. Many people force their families to live second-class lives and endure all the other torments of being broke in order to avoid doing the things that make money and produce income. We become successful by design; we become shirkers, buck passers, and beggars by default.

Whether our income is large or small is not the point. The point is to do our best and learn to handle well what we have, so that everyone with whom we do business will receive genuine satisfaction from his contact with us. That way we ourselves will feel good about what we do. Someone said that we should always treat others as though we were the others. This is a wonderful idea. If we can learn to put it into practice, we will be really great human beings. Yes, one of the most important laws of success is the law of financial respectability.

22 The Law of FREE AGENCY

If they were asked to name the greatest single benefit in life, outside of actual life itself, most people would probably say freedom. The desire for liberty has been the reason that many of the wars have been fought. Every human being wants to be his own master, and every human being owes it to himself sometime in his life to learn to be his own boss, to do his own thinking, to make his own plans, to stand on his own feet, to be his own man.

Yet even in the great land of America, where everyone is politically free, most men are living in economic and occupational slavery where the kind of work available, hours, vacations, and other conditions of employment are determined by someone else. Most human beings are promoting the business of someone else; they are building *his* profits. Most people are like slaves and labor on another man's plantation; they dress the vineyard but someone else is the owner. If the soil is sometimes barren, they are sure of being scourged; if it is fruitful and their care succeeds, they are not usually thanked—they have only done their duty.

You will probably search the list of occupations in vain to find one job that gives as great an opportunity for freedom as you would desire. That would be where one determines his hours, industry, compensation, clients, permanence, and retirement benefits without any interference or control from someone trying to capitalize on his labor.

Of course, freedom is not always an unmixed blessing. It can be a disadvantage, if we are not careful. In the first place, free agency is not always free. It has cost many people their lives, their income, their self-respect. It is free only if we keep on the track.

Did you ever stop to think about the fact that freedom is on a double-entry basis? Like our capitalistic system, it is not a profit system only; it is a profit and *loss* system. It is not a system for obtaining benefits only; it is a system for obtaining benefits and difficulties also. It means punishments as well as rewards. The law of compensation never rests. For every act there must be a consequence. Therefore, freedom may mean failure as well as success. And some people who abuse their privileges and never learn to manage themselves pay dearly for their freedom, for nothing is free, even free agency.

When we enumerate the great freedoms and count our possible benefits, we should remember that most of our troubles come because of our free agency. If we fail, who is to blame? If we lack objectives and fail to plan, no one can be held responsible but ourselves. If we lack industry, fail to study, or fill our personalities full of defects and our efforts full of sloth, we ourselves are responsible. The lack of the ability to manage ourselves is a common weakness in human beings.

The fall of man took place because of freedom. The fall of man is still taking place every day for the same reason: because we are allowed our choice.

There must always be opposites. There must always be alternate choices of good and bad. In spite of the danger, we must be free to choose. For every privilege that we cherish, there is a duty that we must fulfill; for every hope that we entertain, there is a task that we must perform; for every good that we want, there is a sacrifice of comfort and ease that is required. We accept the risk when we accept the opportunity. There is no such thing as something for nothing. Sooner or later, the ledger must be balanced. There is no chance to merely record our credits under a single entry system. We must also record the liabilities.

We have the freedom to be ignorant, the freedom to be poor, the freedom to be unworthy, the freedom to be undependable. These are alternates of the great freedoms, including the freedom to make right choices voluntarily, the freedom to choose the worthwhile and eliminate the undesirable. Freedom is our greatest benefactor—and it can be our greatest disaster. What a terrible thing when we reach the end of the journey if we look back to discover that by our deliberate choice and the consequence of our own acts, we have destroyed ourselves.

Someone has said, "Then lift up your eyes to God. Seek Him whom you resemble. He has created you that you may be like Him." He has made possible to us the great gift of freedom so that we may develop ourselves through the freedom to plan, freedom to think, freedom to work with all our hearts, freedom to manage ourselves, freedom to know, freedom to do, freedom to have, freedom to be. Our problem is that too often we aim too low. Not only should we appreciate our economic freedom, but we should also appreciate our mental, spiritual, and moral freedoms and be prepared to take the full advantage of them. Our freedom coupled with our self-discipline can bring about the most favorable condition of our lives.

23 The Law of FUSION

Did you ever find a tiny fly in a great big bowl of soup? What was your reaction? One thing is certain: *all* of the soup was spoiled.

Now think of a young man of good character associating with men of questionable reputation. What is the verdict? The law says, "You are judged by the company you keep." The part is merged with and judged by the whole. Also, the whole is judged by the part. That is the law of fusion.

Many times we don't separate values, but allow them to run together. They fuse into one another. The personality of the part takes on the character of the whole. If the gummed paper that is stuck full of dead flies in the butcher shop window is in the same area as a steak we might want for dinner, the whole becomes one. It is a little difficult to think of them separately. This is the law of fusion. This is one of the reasons why good merchants dare not mix cheap merchandise with that which is expensive. The price tags are different, but our impressions associate them together, and the good merchandise is spoiled by being too close to the bad.

Now think of our personality qualities. Our personalities are the sum total of our characters, our appearance, our attitudes, our habits, our skills, and our spiritual qualities, which distinguish us from all others. The clothes we wear, the lines in our faces, the tone of our voices, the thoughts we think, the character we have developed by those thoughts, the expression of our eyes, the attractive smile, the magnetic handshake, the company we represent, the friends we associate with—all constitute a part of our personality. We may have fifty personalities, but we make only one impression.

Now suppose one has a dirty collar or dirty fingernails or some other annoying mannerism or personality fault. What is the result likely to be? Probably the same as the flypaper in the butcher shop window. A chain is no stronger than its weakest link, and our entire personality may be neutralized by some small defect. One tiny spot of rot in a great big apple not only classifies the whole apple as rotten, but also endangers all of the other apples nearby.

We are very fortunate if we have a friend who is wise enough and courageous enough to sit down with us occasionally and point out our weak points before this deadly law does too much damage. And we are even more fortunate if we will listen and take heed. Even our appraisal by an enemy is sometimes more accurate than our appraisal of ourselves.

Every person should have some machinery set up for an occasional self-analysis where he attempts to see himself as others see him. What about our speech and our honesty? Are we pulled down by a personality millstone around our necks? Do we have a "dead mouse" in our personality? If we have, the law of fusion will relegate us to a position in the rear of the procession toward success. Remember this: the weak and the strong, the rich and the poor, the ignorant and the well-informed are changing places continually, and whether we are going up or coming down, whether we are eliminating or acquiring defects, and whether this law of fusion will work for us or against us should be a matter of daily and earnest concern.

An important part of a strong physical body is a well-regulated elimination system whereby the waste and impure are regularly being expelled. That is just as necessary to a vigorous, alert, healthy personality. Remember the law of fusion. The whole is judged by the part, and the part is judged by the whole.

24 The Law of GLAD TIDINGS

One of the best ways to learn how to live effectively is to study people and history. Human nature changes very little, and we can learn many valuable lessons in public relations from the past.

For example, an old story tells of a messenger who one day brought good news to an ancient king. The king rewarded him by putting a necklace of gold around his neck, dressing him in the best apparel, inviting him to marry his daughter, and giving him a third of his kingdom.

This story has been reenacted in one form or another in all parts of the world many times. The king didn't seem to pay much attention to who or what caused the good news: he rewarded the one who brought it to his attention. Ancient kings were not bothered much by the inhibitions and restraints of our more complex civilization, so we see human nature acting as it actually is. On the other hand, think what used to happen to the one who brought the king bad news. He was usually imprisoned, banished, or had his head cut off for his pains, according to how bad the news was. Again, what caused the misfortune seemed unimportant. Certainly the messenger was not responsible. He merely told the king about it, but he lost his head just the same.

That doesn't make sense, but many times human nature doesn't seem to make sense. People like to hear good news, particularly about themselves and their own fortunes, and while the practice of cutting people's heads off has been somewhat restricted in our day, yet the effect of ideas on a person's mind and emotions is still pretty much the same. We do not like to hear bad news, and we sometimes feel like hurting the person who gives us any.

Take, for example, someone who is always predicting gloom and failure, or the person who tells us about our faults. He may have the very best of motives. He is trying to help us get rid of our faults. He is trying to build us up. But we would hurt him if we could. We don't get angry because we have the fault; we get angry because somebody tells us about it. It would make more sense if we got mad at the fault and put the gold necklace around the neck of the person who tried to help us overcome it, but that is not human nature. We like the person who tells us good things about ourselves, even if they are false, and we dislike the one who brings us bad news, even if it is true. The people said to Moses, "Tell us good things and we will follow thee." That is a great idea if we are not concerned about the facts.

We should, of course, be on our guard, because many people, knowing of this quality in human beings, try to make the story sound good rather than tell the truth. It has been said that everyone lies to the king. The king usually never hears the bare truth. The news is almost always padded and colored.

In our dealings with people, we often get the urge to put them in their places and to tell them off, but while sometimes that may be necessary, the point to keep in mind is that people like to hear good news. Certainly we ought not to go around peddling gloom and dire predictions of bad events to come. Most of the bad things that we worried about in the past have never happened. There are so many good tidings we can carry, so many nice things about people that we can use to make them happy and build them up. We ought to become carriers of glad tidings. We ought to learn to overlook the faults in people and see only the good. We ought to have interesting things to tell and good things to say about people. It has been said that next to him who first discovers a great truth is him who quotes it.

People like to see us smile, for a smile is an indication of glad tidings in us that makes other people also feel good. We ought to learn to be happy, to be conveyors of enthusiasm, to pass on happiness. We ought to learn interesting and constructive things to tell people about life and its opportunities.

Some 2,000 years ago, the Son of God himself came into the world and brought with him a plan of universal salvation called the gospel. One translation of the term "gospel" is "the good news." The Son of God atoned for the sins of the world, so that all men might have eternal life and eternal happiness. We are redeemed from the bondage of sin and death. The gospel contains the good news of a universal resurrection and the possible eternal glory of the human soul.

We tend to repeat those experiences that give us pleasure. By making success our most pleasant experience, God is trying to entice us on from one success to another until he gets us to the place that he had in mind when he said, "Be ye therefore perfect, even as your Father which is in heaven is perfect." (Matthew 5:48.) To assist in this eternal happiness project, God has announced a program of eternal progression. He has announced that if we will carry this good news to other people, he himself will reward us and give us a glorious intellect and an eternally happy personality. He has announced the rewards for our effectiveness in carrying the good news by saying, ". . . all that my Father hath shall be given unto them." (D&C 84:38.) He projected our future possibilities by saying, "Ye are gods; and all of you are children of the most High." (Psalm 82:6.) What could be more glorious news than the fact that we may become even as God is?

Therefore we return to our thesis that if we would like to have a gold necklace around our neck and own a third of the kingdom and marry the boss's daughter, we should learn about the law of glad tidings, get an interesting command over good news, and then enthusiastically teach it to everybody.

Just think how many good things we have to tell people about God, about the importance of the family, and about themselves! Just think how many good things there are to tell about our right to work and our privilege to develop ambition and skill and usefulness! If we do all of these things well, we will certainly end up finding ourselves sitting on the throne of great power and satisfaction with an eternity of joy and happiness ahead of us.

25 The Law of GRAVITY-UP

A familiar story, first told by Voltaire, tells how a falling apple led Sir Isaac Newton to discover the important law of gravity in the year 1666. The mass of the earth has a mysterious attraction that pulls the apple to it.

This law of attraction is the law that holds the planets in their orbits. Each has an attraction or pull on the others, according to their mass, density, distance, etc., and just as there is an attraction between planets, so there is also an attraction between persons going in the same direction. John Greenleaf Whittier in his quaint Quaker style once said, "Me lift thee and thee lift me, and we'll both ascend together." While that may not be a possibility in the physical world, it is the essence of spiritual, mental, social, and business progress. We lift each other simultaneously; therefore, if one body fails, whether it be a planet or an individual, others in its field of influence are affected accordingly. People, like planets, have orbits. Each person is important to every other person in his magnetic field. If one of us fails, those who have been held in his orbit by attraction may lose their balance.

It is reported that in becoming a millionaire, Andrew Carnegie made thirty-eight other people millionaires. As he worked himself up, he took along with him his suppliers, his partners, and others with whom he did business.

Similarly, when one institution or individual goes broke so that it cuts off its patronage and can't pay its bills, others are consequently dragged down. It is easy to become great in the company of great people. Every great person has a gravity that tends to take others along.

In business, great leaders are placed over us to lift us upward. This is also part of the genius of the church. We hear till we are weary about the temptations of our day; they confront us on every hand. We think of them as the temptations of evil; they are the temptations downward, for they provide the forces that draw us toward Satan and hell. They are the temptations of crime, of atheism, of sin.

Some time ago I looked up the meaning of the word *temptation* and found that to tempt is to arouse a desire for. Desires can go upward even more readily than they can go downward. The beast is thrown down on all fours and thus his vision is cast upon the ground, but we were created upright in the image of our Maker, that we might look up to God. The Author of our salvation has offered us the most exciting temptations upward. If we put ourselves in its magnetic range, the spirit of the gospel will arouse our desires for all of the good things of life, that we might some day become even as God is.

Construction companies have electric magnets to load cars with metal. They set a large magnet over scrap steel and then turn on the current. A mysterious electrical magnetism reaches down and lifts up the pieces of steel and holds them fast to the magnet until they are in position. Then when the current is cut off, the steel falls into the receiving car. This is also the spirit of the gospel. Jesus said, "If I be lifted up . . . I will draw all men unto me." (John 12:32.) Of course, much depends on the quality of the thing being attracted. Even an electric magnet will not pick up a rotten log. This principle may also apply to some people. Greatness has little or no attraction on certain personality qualities, but if the one who is attracted is the right kind of person, he can be pulled up by the greatness of the one who attracts.

We ought to give more thought to ways and means of getting ourselves into greater magnetic influence of great individuals, great ideas, and the spirit of great accomplishment. This may be done in many ways, such as personal association with the right kind of people, reading biographies, the study of great literature.

We talk about "getting ideas." Sometimes ideas get us. Often we entertain an idea that takes possession of us. Abraham Lincoln held in his mind ideas about slavery that would not let him rest, but drew him on and on until he freed the slaves.

Whether we like it or not, like the planets we are each constantly exerting a force on every other person. At the same time that we are being acted upon by the gravity of others, we should be interested in which direction we are pulling and also which way we are being pulled.

Gravity-up can be one of the greatest influences for good in the world. In fact, the fundamental law of the universe is the law of attraction. We are attracted to whatever we truly love and believe in. We tend to become what we think about, and the direction may be either up or down.

One of the best ways to grow is to get the Spirit of the Lord, who is all-wise and all-good, and he also has the greatest lifting power as we get ourselves in his magnetic range. The church, which is made up of righteous members, is like a great constellation, each member being pulled upward by the combined magnetism and good example and personality of every other member. Each is connected to the whole by the faith, ideals, love, and devotion of those making up one of the greatest of all organizations. When you put a magnet close to something it has great power, but when the distance is increased, the power diminishes. For this reason we should stay as close as possible to the Lord and his church and to good people. We should take full advantage of all of this available lifting power.

There is tremendous motivation in a great cause. We form strong attachments to outstanding leaders who move in our orbits. We literally hitch our wagons to the stars, and the law of attraction pulls us upward. Huge numbers of people have worked their way toward their eternal exaltation not only because of the testimonies that they themselves had in the doctrines of truth or even in their testimonies of the Master, but also because they believed the testimony of some great leader who followed the Master, for whom they had genuine love and in whom they had confidence. About these the Lord has said in these latter days, "To some it is given by the Holy Ghost to know that Jesus Christ is the Son of God, and that he was crucified for the sins of the world. To others it is given to believe on their words, that they also might have eternal life if they continue faithful." (D&C 46:13-14.)

There is a most powerful "gravity-up" in the doctrines of salvation and the great religious principles of the Master. This is especially true when we ourselves have a high specific gravity of great devotion to the cause and a vigorous industry in the service of our eternal Heavenly Father. There is a lifting power in thinking up and doing up and imagining up.

"Gravity-up" is one of the important powers for self-improvement. The upward reach is an important part of human personality, foretelling a better life. It is the essence of leadership; it is the heart of religion.

within us active, we are safe. We should find some effective way to help nature by constantly stimulating ourselves. There may be a question in our minds about using some physical stimulants, but mental and spiritual stimulants are necessary to growth, and the more habit-forming they are, the better. It's a part of the principle that if we are not going forward, we will slip backward. When we stop being better, we stop being good. When one avoids struggle, he soon finds that he has changed places with someone who used to play on the second team but who had a stronger struggle urge within him.

It has been said that necessity is the mother of invention. Necessity stimulates our struggle, and one who relaxes in the struggle is soon eliminated. Man is born to struggle. Like the man freezing in the snow, we should keep going. To stop and lie down in a blizzard or in life is the worst thing one can do. No matter what other shortcoming one may have, if he'll just keep on his feet and keep moving in the right direction, he may hope to someday arrive at his destination, and everything will turn out all right.

27 The Law of HEALTH

An old wisecrack says, "I am not in business for my health." However, anyone who has thought about this very much knows that it is not an accurate statement.

The dictionary describes business as that activity which life says one has to do or should do. As soon as one is born, life begins to impose upon him some service or duty or mission that makes up the business of life. When Jesus was twelve years of age, he was aware of this fact, for he said, "Wist ye not that I must be about my Father's business?" (Luke 2:49.)

The business of living is broken up into several vocations or avocations, and whether we like it or not, we are soon confronted with the business of making a living. Everyone becomes a member of a family business—first as a child, then as a husband or wife, then as a parent. Everyone also becomes involved in the business of keeping himself amused and happy, for the scripture says, "Men are, that they might have joy." (2 Nephi 2:25.) But our assigned work must come before almost every other thing, and how we do it contributes greatly to our mental, physical, financial, and moral health. Most of us would not stay healthy or happy for very many pay days if any or all of our business should stop.

People's attitudes about health have undergone many changes over the course of history. Before science proved otherwise, illness was often thought of as the invasion of the body by evil demons. Recently there has grown up a great field of knowledge about our health called psychosomatic medicine, which says that many of the troubles that manifest themselves as physical symptoms have their origin in mental or emotional disturbances.

In one way or another, most people are sick. A person's physical health can be imperiled by certain emotions. If there is bickering and hatred among family members, we are socially sick. If our spiritual appetites degenerate, we become morally sick. If we are possessed by the evil forces of sloth and lethargy, then a whole crowd of troublesome complaints are turned loose upon us. Our emotions are tied up with our success in all areas of our endeavor; consequently, the primary concern of our business is our health.

Mental and nervous breakdowns are usually associated with emotional evils, and breakdowns attributed to overwork are usually caused by our attitudes toward our work and our failure to achieve acceptable standards of excellence. When the evil spirits of frustration, hatred, weakness, and failure are eliminated from our work, then better health will result. Solomon said, "A merry heart doeth good like a medicine." (Proverbs 17:22.) A clear conscience and a sense of righteousness also doeth good like a medicine.

Dr. Karl Menninger of Topeka, Kansas, has said that more people in the United States are mentally ill than are hospitalized for all other diseases and illnesses combined. He says that it is not an overstatement to say that fully 50 percent of the problems of the acute stages of an illness and 75 percent of the difficulties of convalescence have their primary origin not in the body but in the mind of the patient. Work itself does not kill. Laborers do not usually die of heart attacks; it is more frequently the person who is laboring under some unnatural emotional stress where the frustrations and worries settle in his heart. Sickness can be the result of laziness, a guilty conscience, frustrations, and other factors that produce emotions beset with mental conflicts.

Most of these mental, and consequently physical, diseases begin with inertia, lack of planning, idleness, and the habit of running away from our problems. When we fail to study the great spiritual truths and when we fall down in our occupational business, then we are beset with a paralyzing ignorance, and evil spirits overwhelm us, including anxiety, fear, obsession, compulsion, delusions, hallucinations, illusions, and an array of physical complaints stemming from the mind. These are the counterparts of the well-known physical symptoms. When we form bad habits of work or develop unfavorable attitudes about our families, our religion, and our social responsibilities, over a few years' time complexes, emotional deformities, and distortions of attitude result, all of which involve our relations with other people as well as our own feelings and personalities. If these weaknesses are allowed to go far enough, they can lead to mental, physical, and moral breakdowns.

Thus, when we say we're not in business for our health, we are just kidding ourselves. Everyone should be conscious of the fact that he is in business for his health, and he ought to work at it wholeheartedly.

The story is told of an aviator in the Arctic Circle whose plane had crashed. He knew that there was help beyond the hills, but before he had gone very far, he felt a drowsy lethargy overpowering him and he felt that if he could lie down in the soft, warm snow and rest, everything would be all right. As he felt the comfort and peace of his snowy bed, it suddenly dawned on him that he was in the last stages of freezing to death. He jumped to his feet and began running for his life toward the hills, and it wasn't long before the warm blood was churning in his system. All of us are running for our lives, and if we keep our hearts pumping enough blood, we are safe, for while the heart continues to remain sound, all other sicknesses are superficial and temporary.

Our emotions might be compared to the engines of our automobiles. Usually we do not look under the hood until the car stops or begins to sputter, but at that late day, when we try to find and correct the problem, we frequently do not know what we are looking for. When the appendix becomes inflamed, we are warned of the fact by a lot of symptoms. We feel sick to the stomach, have no appetite, are constipated, and there is pain in the abdomen. When we are working and living improperly, we also get some warning symptoms telling us that emotional trouble is imminent. Conflicts begin to arise. We have damaging feelings of guilt and inferiority. We start accusing others, and instead of meeting our problems squarely, we alibi, offer excuses, and think illogically. Then we begin falling down in our business and we may need psychiatric help.

When we are behind in our work, we always hate it. When we are ahead in our work, we always love it. If we abuse our work, we dislike it. If we abuse our families, we dislike them. If we cling to evil, we hate those things having to do with God and righteousness.

Some time ago, a national magazine conducted a survey in which it was found that 75 percent of all people hate their jobs. If they just hated one job the solution would be simple, for they could quit that job and start one that they enjoyed. But, if we ourselves are sick, then we may not like the second job any better than the first, and the third may have just as many failings as the second.

When we get stomach ulcers from our family bickering, that part of our business is in serious trouble, and when we moan about how hard it is for us to live our religion, it is certain that we are not being very devoted to our Father's business. We should take steps to get hold of all of these problems before they get a stranglehold upon us. Any one of these serious emotions that develop because we are not doing our work well may invade the organs of our bodies and leave the patient with several kinds of sickness. Our hate and anger can kill us. Our sloth and lethargy and ignorance can ruin our lives. Our sins against our families can destroy our happiness. And the evil involved in our disobedience to God can destroy our souls.

The mind and emotions are not immune to disorder, and we ought to learn to love our jobs. We learn to love our work by doing it well. Success is antiseptic—it kills all the germs of disease. Sigmund Freud spoke of creating an emotional cathartic, or a purgative medicine, to purify our systems by draining off our pent-up emotions from their unnatural incorporation in the organs of the body. This can best be done by genuine repentance, a turning away from evil, and then launching a vigorous quest for excellence and success in all aspects of our lives.

Disease is a fractional death, and the degree of our health determines the total effectiveness of our lives. The main things for which we are in business are to have life and to have it more abundantly. So let's start this very day and be as businesslike as possible in developing a healthy mind, a healthy spirit, and a healthy personality, incorporated in a healthy body.

28 The Law of the HURDLE

In Aintree, England, just outside Liverpool, each September there is held the Grand National Steeplechase. Forty horses run a race around a course four-and-a-half miles in total length, jumping over thirty-two hurdles, two of which are water jumps, at which the horse and rider must make the hurdle plus a water hazard on the other side.

Usually the first hurdle puts 25 percent of the participants out of the race; another group is eliminated at the second hurdle, and so on through the thirty-two hurdles. The horses and riders are trained to develop strength and skill in getting over these hurdles. Some sixty thousand people attend the race each year, paying as high as $100 for a seat. People like to see anyone, even horses, that can succeed. All sorts of handicaps are placed in the way. The horse never knows what to expect behind the hedge. There may be a moat; he may be "crowded" by other horses; but he must successfully meet each situation as he comes to it. Only a few horses are still in the race at the end of the course. Horses and riders must be good even to be in the race at the finish, and, of course, the winner receives a substantial grand prize.

Life is very much like the Aintree Steeplechase, and if we have the right attitudes, life's obstacles can be immensely arousing and motivating. The pathway of life is generously sprinkled with hurdles to be overcome and difficulties to be surmounted. That's the program, whether we like it or not, and one who is planning the course of his life would do well to learn to appreciate the hurdles and take them into account and prepare himself accordingly. As someone has said, the race is not always to the swift, nor the battle to the strong, but to the one who is still in there fighting at the end of the course.

A motto carved in the Massachusetts School for the Blind says: "Obstacles are things to be overcome." Obstacles make us prepare. They are placed in our way to help us develop strength and skill. The successful man sees opportunities in his obstacles; the unsuccessful man sees obstacles in his opportunities. Certainly to be forewarned is to be forarmed. Hurdles make it possible for the strong, determined, prepared person to work his way up to the front.

It is interesting to see in any group of people how many quit at the first obstacles. Some stick to the job until the second or third hurdle, but only a few develop that quality of stick-to-itiveness and determination that guarantees they will be there at the end. The weakling says how difficult it is for one to live his religion, while the strong person, like Job, says, "Though he slay me, yet will I trust in him. . . ." (Job 13:15.) We should never be a dropout from success. It isn't how many starts we make in life that's important; it is how many times we are there at the finish. Any horse can fall down and quit; it's also very easy for a human being to become discouraged at some little thing that the winner takes in his stride.

Anybody can have a good record for a month, but it's the man who keeps on month after month, year after year, taking all the annoyances and setbacks in his stride, that makes a successful life.

We ought to always keep in mind that hurdles are put in our way for a constructive purpose to develop us. No one ever learns horsemanship on a tame horse. It is not the path of least resistance that builds strength and power and courage and initiative. It is not the peaceful sea that makes the skillful mariner. When the sea is calm, all boats alike show mastership in sailing. It was the north wind that made the Vikings great. Even God himself operates according to the law of the hurdle.

> We ask for strength and God gives us difficulties to make us strong.
>
> We pray for wisdom and God sends us problems, the solution of which develops wisdom;
>
> We plead for prosperity and God gives us brain and brawn to work;
>
> We ask for courage and God gives us dangers to overcome;
>
> We beg for favors and God gives us opportunities.

It's tremendously important that we keep constantly in mind the fact that overcoming our problems and troubles and discouragements is what builds strength. If we have that attitude toward the hurdles of life, we will look on them as helpful benefits and learn to take them as they come, with steady, unruffled composure, and maybe even with substantial, friendly enthusiasm.

Ralph Parlette had a famous lecture on beans and walnuts. He would fill a glass jar half full of little beans and half with big walnuts. Then he would mix them all up together and shake the jar, and the beans would trickle down to the bottom while the walnuts pushed up to the top. Then he would turn the jar upside down and shake it again. All of the beans, which were now on top, would again trickle down to the bottom while the walnuts, which were on the bottom, again worked their way to the top. The same bumps, the same jolting that sent the little beans down also sent the big walnuts up.

This is one of the laws of life that may apply well to our personal success. Some like a little job because it is easy, but the result is that they shrivel up to the size of that which they choose to do. Others like a big job and enthusiastically accept the challenge to make themselves capable of it.

Someone has said that "the Lord fits the back to the burden." If we want a strong back, we should get a big load to carry. It's like striking a balance financially. If our income and outgo do not meet, it is usually a lot better to increase our income than to decrease our outgo.

If we quit when things aren't going as we would like to have them, we will go down like the bean, but if we learn from these jolts in life, we will develop determination and skill to fight our way up to the top. Remember, it's the same shaking in both instances. All of us will have setbacks. Someone has said, "It's nothing against you to fall down flat, but to lie there, that's disgrace." Every person will have hurdles, and some will have handicaps. But all of these are put in our paths to develop our strength and bring us our ultimate happiness. The hurdle is also intended to put those out of the race who otherwise might beat us to the finish line. But if hurdles are good, we should accept them eagerly by running out to meet them.

29 The Law of HYPOCHONDRIA

If you watch television or movies, you know that the most innocent-looking of the suspects often turns out to be the murderer. It is also often true that the hazard we suspect the least is the one that causes our greatest distress. Problems usually lurk unsuspectingly in our own attitudes and imaginations. This might be called life's law of hypochondria.

A hypochondriac is a person subject to imaginary ailments. The dictionary says that hypochondria is a morbid, melancholy anxiety of mind. The personality characteristics in the presence of which hypochondria thrives include inertia, hatred, conflict, jealousy, feelings of inferiority, and the lack of one dominating, single interest.

Sometimes we let our imagination run away from our reason. We magnify little slights and give undue attention to the imperfections of others. Many people will develop "delusions of inference," which are misrepresentations of things they see and hear. We pamper the natural impulse to believe unfavorable things about events and people. We check up on others too closely and do not check up closely enough upon ourselves.

Stable emotions are one of our most valuable possessions. If we indulge the impulse to believe what we want to believe without reference to all the facts, we develop defective reasoning and bring upon ourselves all kinds of imaginary ailments, including mental and physical illnesses.

The abnormal or undisciplined use of emotions and ideas is pretty risky. Few things are more devastating or demoralizing than the deathlike grip of these hypochondrical tendencies.

For generations we have largely overlooked the greatest single cause of human failure and suffering: our emotions. We need far more than a sound body and a keen intellect to get us comfortably through life. We need a sound philosophy of life. When we allow little things, either real or imagined—such as a cross word, rejection, a feeling of lethargy, indisposition, or a few failures—to throw us into a slump, we may become unable to extricate ourselves. We get into the habit of being discouraged or hurt too easily, of seeing offense where none was intended. But even if it was intended, why should we let thoughtless people or even our enemies hurt us? Brigham Young once said that he who takes offense where none was intended is a fool—but he is a fool who takes offense whether it was intended or not.

It is far easier to be envious than industrious, to develop feelings of inferiority than of accomplishment. We imagine a lot of things that are not so. Then we usually become confused when we do not think straight. Nothing is more impoverishing than emotional turmoil, even if the cause is imaginary. The facts are not always as important as what we imagine them to be, or what our attitude is toward them.

Many of us have delusions of persecution, of inferiority, of grandeur, of fear, of illness. We develop the memory of an elephant for every little slight or mistake that someone makes instead of being as generous to the mistakes of others as we are to those we make ourselves.

In training our emotions, a good place to start is to take all the chips off our shoulders and learn to be sincerely friendly to everyone regardless of what his attitudes may be. This business of even loving our enemies is a good idea, for the hater is always more damaged than is the hated.

You probably remember Shakespeare's story of Lady Macbeth. She did a lot of things that were wrong and that she tried to justify, with the result that she didn't think straight. Finally she thrust a dagger into the heart of the sleeping King Duncan, who was a guest in her house, hoping that Macbeth would succeed him in office. These things so preyed on her mind that she finally became demented. She imagined that she still had the blood of the king on her hands even though she washed them a thousand times. But the uncleanness was not on her hands; it was in her mind and heart, where it is much more difficult to get at.

This indicates the extent to which the imagination can take us. It can be stronger and more real than one's eyesight or reason. Macbeth obtained the best physician to try to cure his wife, but the doctor didn't get very far and finally gave up. Then Macbeth said to him:

> Canst thou not minister to a mind diseas'd,
> Pluck from its memory a rooted sorrow,
> Raze out the written troubles of the brain,
> And with some sweet oblivious antidote
> Cleanse with the stuff'd bosom of that perilous stuff
> Which weighs upon the heart?

Then the doctor gave his famous answer when he said: "Therein the patient must minister to himself."

There are certain things that we must do for ourselves, and one is the proper care, supervision, nourishment, and control of our emotions. We must not let ourselves get imaginary ailments. We must practice discipline and train our feelings. When we think a thing, we should act upon it—now. When we make plans, we should carry them out at all costs. Otherwise, these feelings will accumulate inside of us, and we are therefore subconsciously plotting to defeat ourselves.

Without emotional control, our greatest ability is stunted. No one can hurt us but ourselves. It is probable that all of our present imaginary fears and ailments are just as useless as those we worried about last month and last year.

Life's law of hypochondria tells us that a human being has a great tendency to imaginary ailments that he must be on guard against, for most of his problems come in this category. These must be controlled, regulated, and disciplined for a maximum of any success.

30 The Law of IDLENESS

It's a natural law that out of idleness comes weakness. Nature hates idleness in all its forms. She gives continuous life only to those elements which are in use. Tie up an arm or any other part of the body in uselessness and the idle part will soon become lifeless. Reverse the order and give an arm more than normal use, such as the activity engaged in by the blacksmith who wields a heavy hammer all day long, and the arm grows strong.

This law governs physical, mental, spiritual, social, and personality development. It says that the way to growth is activity, whereas the way to death is idleness. Running water purifies itself, but the stagnant water of an inactive pond becomes impure and unhealthy, and so do the cells of a sluggish body or an inactive brain. Laziness is the influence of an inactive mind upon the cells of the body.

Nothing is more common than mental inertia. For every ten people who are physically lazy there are ten thousand with stagnant minds, and stagnant minds are breeding places of fear, ignorance, sin, and crime. The person who is active generates power and breeds courage. The one who has power in his righteousness has little to fear, while the unprofitable servant allows his fear to destroy his faith. We can build up our faith and our industry to where it will eliminate our fear.

One of nature's laws tells us that we should earn our bread before we eat it. When young people want too much ease at the beginning of their lives, they are usually doomed to failure. Rest comes only after it has been earned. When nature sees a young person engaged in inactivity, she assumes that he wishes to become a nobody and immediately begins granting his request.

Many otherwise capable people succumb to this negative law. Often the sons of wealthy families are not properly impressed with the necessity for effort. They try to slide from first base to home plate on their family name, and, in conformity with this law of ease, they lose their inheritance. When one sits too long on his cushions of advantage, he goes to sleep and is soon eliminated from the race.

There are others who fail because their first efforts miscarry, and they lose heart and quit. Success likes to be sought after and wooed. The Master himself said, "Pray without ceasing." Life does not always grant one's first petition. Obstacles are put in our way to strengthen us, but when we misunderstand their purpose and allow them to breed discouragement—that is, when we cannot tell the difference between temporary setbacks and permanent failure—then we turn off our effort and succumb to the penalties of the law of idleness.

Temporary failure is nature's great crucible in which she burns the dross from the human heart and so purifies the man that he can stand harder usage. It is said that fortune often disappoints him whom she secretly anoints. A poet has written:

> How she hammers him and hurts him,
> And with mighty blows converts him.

Hard hammering is always necessary to make the finest steel. Because of the law of opposition, it is necessary that people be acquainted with obstacles and rough going. Most men develop faster after they understand opposition, which arouses them to greater action. Our strength grows out of our weakness. Not until we are pricked and stunned and shot at is our indignation awakened. When he is punished and pushed, tormented and defeated, a person has a chance to learn something. And when we cease to look for a life of ease, we have a chance to go places.

Naturally we would all like to have someone give us detailed directions as to how to succeed and then give us the push that would carry us across the goal line. No one can succeed for us except ourselves, and no two persons find the same way to the goal. Each must find his way there by himself. Effort and struggle—both mental and physical—are the way by which we achieve. Life was never intended to be just a pleasure trip or a downhill ride. It is an uphill journey. It is a conquest, a long series of difficulties and obstacles to be mastered.

Don't worry about getting tired, for weariness usually does not come from overwork, but from lack of interest in what you are doing. The muscles never grow fast until we give them some heavy usage. The possession of potential power and the use of it are two different things. The use of our strength makes us powerful, while the pursuit of easy things makes us weak. It is seldom the work that makes us tired. More likely we are tired because of the work we have left undone.

When things are really clicking for us, we seldom get tired, and we can then accomplish many times the work we previously did. Fatigue is caused not by work but by worry, frustration, and resentment. The kite always rises against the wind, not with it. The strongest oak tree of the forest is not the one that is protected from the storm and hidden from the sun, but the one that stands in the open where it is compelled to struggle for its existence against the winds and rains and scorching sun. A great oak struggling in the wind sends down a stronger root upon the windward side. In the same way, the Lord fits the human back to the burden. When we are struggling, we grow. When we retire so that we can take things easy, we are usually on our way out.

The law of success says that idleness always leads to deterioration and death, and these should be avoided by those who would be strong.

31 The Law of INSTINCTS

Wouldn't it be interesting if we could see all the component parts that make up a human being and understand each part as one understands the parts of his automobile, and then have an instrument panel containing all the operation controls. Of all the scientific marvels of the atomic age, no invention has yet come close to equaling the devices that nature has installed in a human being, most of which are so complicated that they defy the most scientific investigation.

For example, the brain of a man is about the size of one's two hands. It is 70 percent liquid, which is constantly changing, and yet it can contain within itself more knowledge than might be in a library of thousands of books. Just think of all the pictures and knowledge of many subjects that are filed in the memory. Or think of the complicated nervous system with all its automatic devices and controls. When a line of communication is cut, it mends itself.

Just think of the temperature controls. The body temperature of a person in Alaska is 98.6 degrees—which is exactly the temperature of a man on the equator. Our temperature in a hot room is 98.6 degrees, and when we go out into a cold blizzard, it is still 98.6 degrees.

Here's another example of the inventive wonder of nature. A bird is hatched out of an egg, and, without going to college or taking courses in home economics or physiology, in its first year of life it goes through all the complications of becoming a parent. It knows exactly how to build a home, hatch eggs, and provide a living for itself and its young. A bird has not heard a single lecture on geography and knows nothing about winter snows; it has no addresses, road maps, compass, weather reports, or electronic steering devices. Yet long before cold weather puts in its appearance, the bird starts a long southern migration on exactly the right day.

We might compare the instincts of a one-year-old mother bird with those of a one-year-old human being. By means of magic powers some of the lower forms of life are completely able to begin their life's work a few hours after their birth, whereas man has the longest period of infancy and dependency known in the universe.

Nature has equipped animals with a set of instincts from which they are not allowed to deviate during their entire lives. Beasts have many of the same organs, the same sensations, the same perceptions that we have, but they are the same today as they were in the beginning of the world. One generation of animals passes no mental accomplishment on to the next. After a few months of life, they show no improvement. But with man this is not so. He was formed for infinity, and to prevent him from remaining without improvement, God has implanted within him a sense of ambition and of satisfaction arising from the contemplation of the excellency of his accomplishment. Man is more ignorant in the earliest age of his life, but he is given an additional and exclusive sense called reason. We can stop and think things out instead of leaving our machinery set on automatic control.

Because of this quality to learn new things and to remember what he learns, man makes his progress accumulative, for he not only derives advantage from his own experience, which the animals do not, but he also can learn from his predecessors. He also has access to the knowledge of the ancients in the books they have bequeathed to him.

Probably because of our reason we have not paid as much attention to the importance of our own instincts as we should have done, and because of this neglect, the effectiveness of our instincts has been reduced somewhat. But they are still very important and could, if understood and cultivated, be far more useful to us.

Instincts are placed in human personality for a good purpose, and an important part of our education is to recognize, understand, and cultivate these powerful and valuable inherent tendencies. Some of the more prominent and fundamental of these instincts are:

1. The instinct for self-preservation
2. The sex instinct
3. The instinct for acquisition and the desire for ownership
4. The instinct to love
5. The combative instincts—envy, rivalry, revenge, hate
6. The parental instinct
7. The instinct of curiosity
8. The instinct of fear
9. The desire for approval
10. The instinct to imitate

The machine age has taught us a great deal about automatic controls, safety devices, automatic thermostats, and so forth. Probably nowhere do they operate more perfectly than in a human being. For example, if we go without food for a certain period, a pang that we call hunger is automatically produced that incites us to seek food. When we have eaten, the feeling ceases until our body again requires nourishment. Hunger not only tells us when to eat, but also what to eat. If we have had too much of one kind of food, we have a feeling that we want some other kind of food. By this process, our physical organism is preserved.

We have another instinct that informs us of fatigue. When we work too hard or too long or run too fast to the point where we are endangering our health, a pain called fatigue tells us we should rest. Again, if it were not for this timely warning, we would get into trouble.

Let's look at some of these instincts. For example, the sex instinct is largely inoperative until we get to an age when nature intended that it should be brought into play for a constructive purpose; then, as if by magic, there it is.

Or consider the instinct of fear. Almost everything in the world we do is because of fear. We go to school because we're afraid of being ignorant. We work because we're afraid of being broke. We practice the laws of health because we're afraid of sickness. We watch our conduct because we're afraid for our reputations. When we fall short in some of these areas, nature produces in us a sensation that cannot be described but that everybody recognizes. We call it fear. And when we get ourselves properly prepared, the warning ceases.

Can you think of anything more wonderful? If we would cultivate our instincts, we would become far more effective. We are driven by our passions and restrained by our consciences, all for our control and welfare. When we stop to think how all of the emotions, the motives, the feelings, and almost everything we do are tied up with powerful instincts, we see how necessary it is to study them and find out as nearly as we can how they operate.

Every human being has an almost all-powerful God instinct, an upward reach, a yearning for better things, a striving to be as God is. He himself has said, "Ye are gods; and all of you are children of the most High." (Psalm 82:6.) He starts us on this upward climb by saying, "Be ye therefore perfect, even as your Father which is in heaven is perfect." (Matthew 5:48.) We develop this God instinct by understanding truth and practicing unwavering obedience to God's commands. None of us will ever reach a maximum of effectiveness until we learn to understand as much of these powerful forces in our God-given human instincts as it is possible to understand.

Just as great leaders learn how to play on the keys of these instincts in others to produce desired objectives, so we also must learn how to effectively direct the natural forces and instincts in ourselves. They are powerful causes of action and may open up to us the greatest desired success in ourselves.

32 The Law of LOVE

One of the most thrilling stories from any era of time is the old story from Grecian mythology of Pygmalion and Galatea. Pygmalion was a sculptor from Cyprus, and like all great artists, he loved his work. Then came the time when he was to create the masterpiece of his life. In deathless ivory he would carve the statue of a beautiful woman and show the human form and personality at its best. Pygmalion worked devotedly and untiringly week after week until the work was finally finished. So great was the effort and devotion, skill and love that Pygmalion lavished upon his work that the gods ordained that the statue should have the power to breathe and move. As she stepped down off the pedestal, Pygmalion called her Galatea, and then Pygmalion married his work.

The story of Pygmalion can be the story of every person, for the work of every person who falls in love with his work shall live.

Love is the most pleasant and profitable of all human experiences. Robert Southwell said, "Not where I breathe, but where I love, I live." Love is the universal peg on which the world is hung. It is the motive power that makes everything go. It is what keeps a person on the job when he might otherwise be discouraged and worn out. Love sweetens the most ordinary enterprises.

One woman reported the doctors as saying that her husband had lived with a particular incurable disease longer than anyone else had ever lived with it. The reason was that the couple's intense love for one another would not let him die. Love is the universal feeling of all human beings to be desired. It is highly developed in some, poorly developed in others.

To different people the word *love* may mean different things. The dictionary says that love is a complex emotion or feeling of affection or regard that causes one to appreciate, to take pleasure or delight in. Love is devotion, affection, attachment.

Some of the ancients believed that the soul of the lover lived in the body of the object loved. We sometimes express a similar idea by saying that one has his heart in his work. Love is like a clinging vine: it can be trained to attach itself and be supported by many of those things that it comes in contact with. Many people make the most serious mistake of their lives by leaving undeveloped and untrained this great power, allowing it to attach itself to whatever it comes in contact with, whether of good or evil.

If a gardener does not train a climbing vine, it climbs and clings indiscriminately and some of the most desirable of all possible results are lost. It is even more important that a human being should learn to climb upward by falling in love with the proper person.

Recently a woman came to talk about some of her marital problems. Three different men had proposed marriage to her. She had been married on two previous occasions and her husbands had been brutal, lazy, immoral, unthoughtful, and selfish, and she didn't want to make another mistake, so she was seeking someone to assist her in making the right choice. Because she seemed to have a larger than ordinary supply of prospective husbands, I asked her the secret of her popularity. She indicated that she picked men up at the bars where they had gone to drown their sorrows and forget their failures. It was suggested that if she wished to avoid a repetition of her previous mistakes, she might do well to seek men with a different kind of background and who were growing up in a different kind of soil.

Each of us ought to give a great deal of consideration to what and whom we are going to fall in love with, and then we should get ourselves into those locations and attitudes where the particular things we seek might be more readily available. We must develop the power to act in our own interests and learn the details of what it should be put in contact with and how we can train it to cling only to those objects that are desirable.

We develop a lot of unnecessary worries, fears, and hates that repel us in our attempts at solid attachments. Many people go out of their way to find a complicated or expensive way of doing things, when the simple, inexpensive, and obvious way is right under their noses.

The magnificent story of Pygmalion, written so many ages ago, has been adapted in our own day in a play by George Bernard Shaw. In this play Professor Henry Higgins took a common flower girl off the street and made her into a lady. The possibilities of this idea have not yet been exhausted, and we might make an adaptation to suit our own needs.

The life of unprotected iron is short, for it has one deadly enemy—oxygen. To preserve the strength of iron, beams and metals in steel frames are treated with graphite paint. A simple coat of paint can protect the strength of skyscraper iron and make it last for many years. It is also the power and function of love to protect our work and our lives so that the destructiveness of failure and deterioration may not enter.

It has been said that we should even love our enemies. That was certainly not said for the benefit only of our enemies, for the hater is far more seriously damaged than the hated. But we can turn them both into friends by putting around them a coat of love that will supply them with the strength and utility of iron. Why should we always be so concerned about getting even with people, when it always does damage to both them and us? Napoleon was by no means an ideal character, but he had superb indifference to personal animosity. When someone questioned his judgment in appointing one of his critics to an important office, he expressed surprise. "What do I care what he thinks of me," Napoleon demanded, "so long as he can do the work." Benjamin Disraeli had the same calm superiority to personal resentment. He said, "I never take trouble to be avenged." Abraham Lincoln kept two of his worst enemies in his cabinet because he wanted the advantage of their frank criticism. With this idea in mind, someone has said, "Unwilling friend, let not thy spite abate; help me with thy scorn and strengthen me with hate."

Will Rogers said, "I never met a man I didn't like." That's why Will Rogers was also loved by everyone and was thought to be one of the greatest men of his time.

If biography and history teach anything, it is that great men have almost always refused to poison their spirits with vindictiveness and hate. It's far cheaper to bear a wrong than to try to avenge it. If people have wronged you, it will do you no harm to give them a chance to forget it. To be hated may be annoying; to hate is a calamity. Someone has said that you don't get stomach ulcers because of what you eat; you get stomach ulcers because of what is eating you.

There is nothing so hygienic as friendship. To love and be loved kills discord, nervousness, and lengthens life; it means an even pulse, clear eyes, good digestion, and sound sleep. We can get along without being loved, but we can't afford to live without loving. Falling in love is the beginning of all wisdom, all sympathy, all passion, all art, all religion, and in a large sense is the one thing worth doing.

Consider how much more pain is brought on us by the anger and vexation we feel over some wrong acts than by the acts themselves. In the make-up of some rare and fortunate people, resentment, fear, prejudice, and hate do not exist. Some people accept slights, ingratitude, and stupidity as a matter of fact, realizing that those things are universal and that it is our business not to imitate either rogues or fools.

It is true that it is not always easy to love, but we must not let a few obstacles throw us off our course. The very nature of love demands opposition and obstacles, just as it is the intermittent or obstructed current that gives power. One can't subdue an enemy by force or hate. The only way to destroy an enemy is by love; he then becomes our friend. We shouldn't worry too much about what anybody else may think of us or who gets the credit. Our main concern should be what we think of him, because what we think of him will be what he will think of us. If you have ever had anyone that you mortally hated, you know that you have never been in so much misery.

Now let us think of the person we love. We admire everything about him, and the world is full of sunshine. When we buy a great painting we hang it in the best possible light; in a similar manner, people and situations we come into contact with should always be considered in their best light. Just think what a difference it would make if we were as generous in overlooking other people's faults as we are our own!

We ought to love people and do things for them. Love is magic. It does wonderful things. If we have love in our heart, it will not be long before it will be on our face, in our eyes, in our footstep, in our handshake. There can be no secrets in life and morals, because nature has so provided that every beautiful thought we know and every precious sentiment we feel shall shine out in our face so that all who will may see.

We should all quit holding grudges and remembering slights. We need to learn to love our job so that the work we do will be the play we love. We need to learn to love our enemies. And we should always remember that for everyone who falls in love with his work, his work shall live.

> Three friends have I:
> He who loves me,
> He who hates me,
> And he who is indifferent to me.
>
> He who loves me teaches me tenderness,
> He who hates me teaches me caution,
> And he who is indifferent to me
> Teaches me self-reliance.

33 The Law of LOYALTY

The sunflower has been called the symbol of loyalty. A story is told of a ship that had been torpedoed at sea, and the crew deserted the ship for the lifeboats. Only two persons remained—the commanding officer, who had been blinded by the explosion, and his personal attendant, who had served him faithfully for many years. The captain, true to the tradition of the sea, had decided to go down with the ship, dressed in his smartest uniform and with all of the flags flying. The faithful servant had stood silently at the side of his blind master without making his presence known until all the lifeboats were filled and out to sea.

As the water gradually rose to their knees and then their waists, the captain urged his aide to save himself. The servant then told his now blinded master the story of the sunflower, the symbol of loyalty. The sunflower follows the sun, not only in the early hours when the day is young, but also at the day's zenith when the heat is the most intense. The sunflower looks directly into the sun in the morning, is constant and steadfast throughout the long afternoon, and, as the sun declines, follows it until it finally disappears into the horizon.

The servant concluded, "That is loyalty." Then, just before the ship reared up on its end to plunge with its two occupants to the bottom of the sea, the servant added, "The sunflower follows the sun; you go down with your ship, and I go down with you."

Super people are usually people with super loyalties. Loyalty is the spirit of Nathan Hale, who at age twenty-one said, "I only regret that I have but one life to lose for my country." As a consequence of his loyalty, he lives forever in the hearts of his countrymen. Job said of God, "Though he slay me, yet will I trust in him." (Job 13:15.)

Loyalty makes ours those things to which we are loyal, while disloyalty removes them from us. Whether or not anyone knows of our disloyalty is really beside the point. The real point is the effect it has upon us. When these super loyalties are applied toward one's company, his family, his church, or himself, he is marked for leadership and top honors, whereas a menial is a person who is disloyal to his work. The law of loyalty says that we must think loyalty and then put it into action.

The legions of Caesar, upon entering his service, swore to hold "the life of Caesar dearer than all else." There used to be a similar custom in Spain: when a commander was slain in battle, those who attended his person continued to fight until they had all died with him. Socrates said, "What ever place thou assignest me, sooner will I die a thousand deaths than desert it." When we undertake a task, if it is worthwhile, we might do well to swear allegiance to it, even as Caesar's soldiers did to Caesar.

The dictionary defines loyalty as follows: "to be constant and faithful in any relationship, implying trust or confidence." If we are loyal, most people will overlook many of our errors, but if we are not loyal, nothing else we do will help much. To be disloyal is to be faithless, false, or inconstant to one's obligations.

Elbert Hubbard said, "If you work for a company, in heaven's name work for it." We shouldn't be afraid to get a little bit excited about our business or about our company when we talk about it. An ounce of loyalty is worth a pound of cleverness. One who is loyal radiates enthusiasm. It lights up his whole personality. It puts a sparkle in his eyes, a light in his expression, and money in his pocket. Loyalty is a far greater incentive than money.

If a person would inspire the confidence and trust of those with whom he associates, he would be loyal to them. He must not be inconstant like the weathercock, which changes its mind at every new breeze. There are many people who live in America who are not loyal to America. If their loyalties are in some other place, they ought to go there quickly so they could without reservation be loyal and enthusiastic, because these traits make a personality rich and strong.

In the absence of loyalty, there is no progress. The story is told of a student who went to a great university where he developed a bad attitude about his school. He overemphasized in his mind some shortcomings of the institution and listened to the other students who were disgruntled. He tried to accumulate all of their complaints in his one personality. As a consequence, he lost confidence in the university, and the university lost its power to help him. Who was hurt? Not the university; not the enthusiastic, loyal students; only the student who had become negative and disloyal.

No one is perfect. If we are looking for faults, we can find them everywhere, but because an institution or a country or a church or our family may not be perfect, we shouldn't let that make us sour. If we need help to be loyal to others, we should just think of some of our own mistakes. We mustn't become gripers, critical, or bearers of tales. If we do, we are getting dangerously close to a violation of the law of loyalty.

One who is disloyal or unloyal, one who is a troublemaker, one who always has a bellyache is the one who is marked for the earliest elimination in the race for success, for the law of loyalty says we must be loyal or be eliminated. We cannot safely tamper with unloyalty or disloyalty.

It's a lot of fun to believe in our company, its leaders, our associates, and ourselves. It's a lot of fun to be loyal to them. It's a noteworthy accomplishment to be a loyal American, a loyal disciple of the Master, a staunch friend, a constant citizen, a faithful family member. It's a lot of fun to believe in people, to believe in God, and to believe in oneself. A super loyalty is the greatest mark of a leader, and one doesn't need to wait for the formality of being elected to leadership. All one needs to do to become a leader is to lead. Leadership comes at the discretion of the leader.

Alexander the Great was a man as infirm and vulnerable as many other men, but his soldiers cried out to him to lead them boldly forward, for while they had such a king, they defied both weariness and thirst and they looked upon themselves to be little less than immortal. Such is the power of loyalty. Remember: "The sunflower follows the sun." "Loyalty is not a gift; it is a superb accomplishment."

34 The Law of MATURITY

At the beginning of this century a man named Stanford Benet made a study of the fact that all people do not mature at the same rate. He discovered that at a certain chronological age, the normal child can be expected to do certain things. If at that age the child is still unable to do the expected things, he is termed retarded; that is, he is younger on the mental scale of growth than he is on the scale of physical growth. If he can do more than the normal, his mental age is advanced. Benet invented the "Intelligence Quotient," a table by which to measure mental age.

Later psychologists extended their explorations into the emotional and social areas of the individual's life. Here too it was discovered that chronological age is not always the correct basis for measuring maturity. A woman of thirty may be on the emotional or social level of the average fifteen-year-old. Chronologically she is an adult, but her emotional reactions are still those characteristic of adolescence. A boy of ten may have a sense of responsibility and steadiness of purpose that go normally with twenty years.

Not all adults are adult. Many who look grown-up on the outside may be childish on the inside. A man of twenty-five may have the self-centered outlook of a five-year-old, while a youth of fifteen may be more manly than his grandfather.

The difficulty a person has when he remains immature emotionally is that he cannot use his highly developed intellect effectively in other fields. He is held back because of neurotic fears, prejudices, fanaticisms, and unreasoning hates. If he has emotional roadblocks that have prevented him from reaching emotional maturity, it is impossible for him fully to utilize those aspects of his personality that are developed.

The forms that adult childishness take are almost infinite in number, and they exist not only in those unfortunates who have to be confined to institutions. One of the difficulties about this situation is that in grown-up child minds, immaturities are almost invariably disguised from the individuals themselves. Such immaturities indicate that the adult is still trying to work out his problems by childish means, and some individuals at forty are still getting their way by using methods common in young children.

It has been said that "where there is no vision, the people perish." But we might add that where there is no maturity, there is no vision. Many of the evils of our lives come not from any deep-seated evil within us, but from ungrown-up responses to life. The most dangerous members of our society are those adults whose powers and influence are mature but whose motives and responses are infantile.

Maturity in one area of our lives promotes maturity in other areas, while immaturity in one area promotes immaturity in other areas. It is another example of the old fact that "he that hath, to him shall be given: and he that hath not, from him shall be taken away even that which he hath." (Mark 4:25.)

Knowledge alone is not enough to save us from confusion and failure. It is most effective only when it is held in constellation with other powers. To help us gain increased self-confidence through the experience of solving problems correctly, we must have all of these powers and abilities growing together toward maturity. Everyone is immature to some degree, as indicated in the following list:

1. If one makes no effort to gain knowledge, he is immature. The adult may have within himself a hidden emotional urge to leave books alone. In his unconscious mind he may still be fighting out one of the major battles of

his childhood, and he may be settling the issue now as he tried to settle it in his school days.

2. A person remains immature whatever his age as long as he thinks of himself as being an exception or different from other human beings. Everyone has problems, disappointments, and weaknesses.

3. A person is immature if he regards the support of his family as a kind of trap into which he has somehow been caught.

4. The person who cannot settle down, who remains a vocational drifter or who wants the prestige of a certain type of work but resents the preparation and routines that go with it, is immature in his sense of adult functioning.

5. It has been said that the boy's will is the wind's will—constantly changing. Unfortunately, many adults without any legitimate reason are as veering and unstable as children. The journey from childhood and irresponsibility belongs legitimately to childhood, when the sense of long-range cause and effect is still rudimentary.

6. The feeling of helplessness is, likewise, a mark of immaturity. Sometimes an adult remains a child if in his youth he is constantly supported by others and has never been forced to exercise his faculties and thus grow up.

7. Many of us fail to mature properly because we have been shielded from the real problems of life. Sometimes it takes such great issues as war or depression or calamity to bring about maturity. Sheer helpless ignorance is childishness. Hostility is childish. Only the immature person takes a perversely hostile attitude toward the world, wears a chip on his shoulder, is suspicious of others, has an elephant's memory for past slights, enjoys other people's defeats, is prone to exaggerate, angers easily, and in response to small irritations enjoys "telling someone off."

8. It is immature to draw conclusions before all the facts are in.

9. Another sign of immaturity is a "hopscotch" mind that is continually jumping from one thing to another. A child wants everything it sees, and it drops one toy after another as each new thing is offered.

10. Children often expect fulfillment of their ambitions by dreaming. This is a pattern of psychological immaturity that often carries over into adulthood. Fulfillment of ambitions by a planned, sustained program of action distinguishes psychological maturity. In the helplessness and ignorance of childhood, we often run away from our problems. Escapism in adult life is childish.

11. The child meekly accepts his lot, whereas an adult believes he is the master of his fate. Emotionally, many people prefer to remain dependent children or flitting adolescents.

12. The person with the mature mind tries to foresee consequences and to eliminate as best he can the personal equation that makes him see what his fears and hopes tell him to see. A mature adult imagines better ways of doing things that never occur to a child. Avoiding issues or sidestepping problems does not build a mature mind.

A great deal of knowledge about the human mind and character has been discovered by psychologists, psychiatrists, physicians, anthropologists, and sociologists, and we should take some pains to make this knowledge available to ourselves. Not to avail ourselves of this knowledge means that we are misshaping, not shaping, our lives.

At no time is the adult exempt from the obligation of practicing maturity. We have a childhood of some length at the beginning of our lives and then usually regress into a "second childhood" at the end of life. This is natural and to be expected. But to have a perpetual and eternal childhood, running from one end of life to the other, is a condition to be studiously avoided.

A human being is a multitude of abilities, senses, tastes, emotions, instincts, aptitudes, likes and dislikes, all of which should be individually identified, sought out, nourished, controlled, and trained. To remain immature in any one of these tends to keep us immature in others. We should learn to develop and control our instincts as well as our intellects.

Occasionally we should check up on ourselves. Here are some good questions we might ask:

1. How old am I mentally?
2. How old am I emotionally?
3. How old am I financially?
4. How old am I socially?
5. How old am I spiritually?
6. How old am I occupationally?

Heredity does not mean that a trait must go unchanged and unchangeable from the beginning to the end of one's life. Certainly it is not so with respect to mental, social, and emotional characteristics. We should study our situations with maturity, and watch out for childish traits in others and in ourselves. If we can first identify, then isolate, then eliminate the causes of immaturity, we will be on our way. One of our main duties and responsibilities of life is merely to grow up.

35 The Law of MODIFICATION

Everyone born into the world immediately begins that all-important journey of life that, so far as our present consideration is concerned, begins at birth and ends with death. This short period of mortality is the most important part of our eternal lives. We all passed the requirements of our first estate, and each one earned the right to receive God's great promise when he said, "Those who keep their second estate shall have glory added upon their heads for ever and ever." (Abraham 3:26.) Certainly nothing could be more important than the fact that our eternal lives will depend upon how we spend these few short years of mortality.

In the meantime, there are many rules and guidelines that can be of great help to us if we learn them in time. One is the law of modification. The dictionary says that a modification is an alteration.

One of the most important applications of the word *modification* is found in the way it applies to human beings. It is an interesting thought that everything we think, everything we do, and everything that is done to us modifies us. Tennyson said, "I am a part of all that I have met." Another writer said, "I can no more remember the books I have read than the meals I have eaten, yet each is a part of all that I am." When one drop of ink is placed in a glass of water, the make-up of the water is no longer the same; and when a new emotion passes through our nervous sytems, our function from that point onward and forever will be different than it otherwise would have been. Shakespeare said, "Refrain tonight; and that shall lend a kind of easiness to the next abstinence: the next more easy; for use almost can change the stamp of nature." (*Hamlet,* Act III, scene 4.)

All growth is modification. When food is taken into our digestive systems, our chemistry is changed. When a new thought runs through our minds, it makes a little groove or engram, and if we think the same kinds of thoughts that went through the brain of Thomas Edison or Henry Ford or William Shakespeare or the apostle Paul or Jesus of Nazareth, we will then tend to think a little more as they did. By this process of modification, we can send ourselves from the bottom to the top of life, or we can come from the top down to the bottom.

When we think negative thoughts, we develop negative minds. When we think depraved thoughts, our minds become depraved. On the other hand, we can think the kinds of thoughts that God himself thinks, and then we tend to become as he is and to think celestial thoughts.

Edward Dyer once said:

> My mind to me a kingdom is;
> Such present joys therein I find
> That it excels all other bliss
> That earth affords or grows by kind.

When we think of wise men, a name that often comes to mind is Solomon. Solomon's father was King David of ancient Israel, the king who spent his lifetime fashioning a great nation, and young Solomon ascended the throne when he was just a teenager. Solomon went to Gibeon and offered sacrifices to the Lord, and the Lord appeared to him in a dream by night and said, "Ask what I shall give thee.

> And Solomon said, Thou hast shewed unto thy servant David my father great mercy, according as he walked before thee in truth, and in righteousness, and in uprightness of heart with thee. . . .
>
> And now, O Lord my God, thou hast made thy servant king instead of David my father: and I am but a little child; I know not how to go out or come in. . . .

> Give therefore thy servant an understanding heart to judge thy people, that I may discern between good and bad: for who is able to judge this thy so great a people?
>
> And the speech pleased the Lord, that Solomon had asked this thing.
>
> And God said unto him, Because thou hast asked this thing, and hast not asked for thyself long life; neither hast asked riches for thyself, nor hast asked the life of thine enemies; but hast asked for thyself understanding to discern judgment;
>
> Behold, I have done according to thy words: lo, I have given thee a wise and an understanding heart; so that there was none like thee before thee, neither after thee shall any arise like unto thee.
>
> And I have also given thee that which thou hast not asked, both riches, and honour; so that there shall not be any among the kings like unto thee all thy days.
>
> And if thou wilt walk in my ways, to keep my statutes and my commandments, as thy father David did walk, then I will lengthen thy days. (1 Kings 3:5-14.)

As a result of this great endowment, the scripture says, "And all the earth sought to Solomon, to hear his wisdom, which God had put in his heart." (1 Kings 10:24.)

But in his later years Solomon did not keep the commandments of the Lord. With all of his great natural advantages, even Solomon, with all of his wisdom, disobeyed the Lord. He married many idolatrous women and sacrificed to their idols on the high places that he had erected for them. Then Solomon died an idolater, very much out of favor with God. The scriptures say that he did evil in the sight of the Lord and went not fully after the Lord as did David, his father. The Lord was angry with Solomon because his heart was turned from him, though he had appeared to him twice and had commanded him concerning going after other gods, but he kept not the Lord's commandments.

Solomon, the once wonderful young man who had started out at the top in his favor with God, had been modified by evil influences until he was responsible for scuttling the whole program of the Lord in ancient Israel.

If we would like to have a more exalted example of modification that can take place in us, we might go back to the council in heaven and get acquainted with Lucifer, the brilliant son of the morning, who stood so close to God in the council in heaven that he aspired to be the Savior of the world. When he was not accepted, he rebelled against God and was cast out of heaven, and as he has continued to fight against God, all good has gone out of him and he has become pure evil; his final end will be complete and permanent banishment.

While these cases are spectacular, yet they apply to us in proportion to the good or evil of which we permit ourselves to become a part. There is a law of physics that says that to every action there is an equal and opposite reaction, and if we do the works of Lucifer, to that extent we smother out the good from our lives and become as Lucifer.

On the other hand, we think of many people who have started in humble circumstances and as they have grown to maturity, they have added to their lives industry, faith, righteousness, courage, ambition, and godliness—and they have climbed to great heights of accomplishment and honor.

Those who qualify for the celestial kingdom will be entitled to live forever with God. Every good thought we think modifies our lives. Every time we do a good deed, we are changed. Every time an emotion, good or bad, runs through our hearts, we are changed, and we will never be the same again.

The God of creation has set before his children celestial glory as their primary objective, and the great laws of free agency and opposites indicate that if we can rise to that highest goal, we can also sink to the lowest hell. Everything we do throughout life tends to push us toward one of these goals. We must allow no exceptions in our pursuit of righteousness. By making success a habit, we may so modify ourselves that we may be eligible for celestial glory.

36 The Law of OBJECTIVES

One law of success says that we must first have an objective. Before we set out on any journey, we ought to know something about where we want to go, how we are going to get there, and when we expect to arrive. With a tightly held objective, clearly visualized and greatly desired, success becomes easier.

For example, until the year 1926, no woman had ever swum the English Channel. Then an automobile company offered a red Buick convertible automobile and $2,500 in cash to the first woman who would accomplish this feat. A nineteen-year-old American girl named Gertrude Ederle wanted that automobile, so she decided to swim the English Channel in order to get it. Part way across, her strength began to give out, and she felt she couldn't swim one more stroke. But as she lay there waiting to be taken out of the water, she closed her eyes and before her imagination passed this red Buick convertible. This firing of her imagination gave her a new surge of strength, and she didn't stop again until she felt under her feet the sands of the opposite shore. This visualization of the objective made her the first woman to swim the English Channel, and without this tightly held objective, success would have been impossible.

In view of the magic motive power within ourselves, it seems unbelievable that many people should spend their lives trying to be successful and yet not have definite, well-defined, clear-cut daily, weekly, and monthly goals. This should be accompanied by a written record against which their daily performance may be measured.

The Roman emperor Maxim beheld in a dream a young maiden so beautiful that upon awakening he declared that he could not live without her. For years his envoys scouted the world in search of her. He knew what he wanted and had the determination to attain his objective, and so all his efforts were bent in that direction until it was accomplished.

So it is with each of us. We need an objective. We need something to tie to. We need a clear-cut ideal. We need a star to steer by. It has been said that "genius is the power to visualize the objective," and in order to visualize the objective, we must get it clearly and definitely in mind. We must have a focus point toward which we may work with all our might. If one is continually changing his objective, there can be very little progress. For the person who does not know where he is going, no winds are favorable, and if he has no time table in mind, his arrival may be both indefinite and uncertain.

Take a small electric magnet and see how it loses its strength as the distance is increased from the thing to be attracted. That is also true with our objectives. Unless we give it some special treatment, an objective beyond the reach of our present needs seems to us to be unimportant. This is a dangerous illusion if we are without the ability to compensate for this deception. Many people would trade their mansion in heaven for the smallest convenience in the present.

We can overcome this handicap placed upon us by learning to "prelive" the objective. That is, we should first get an objective; second, make it as definite as possible by writing out exactly what we want to accomplish weekly, monthly, and annually, as well as figuring out where we want to be forty years from now; and third, let our minds run ahead and live the last end first.

We may begin by cataloguing in our imagination all the pleasures of our future objectives. Think of the advantages we may obtain for ourselves by not allowing ourselves to become discouraged. Think how happy and proud our spouses and children are of us. Think of the honors we will have from our company and the great regard in which we will be held in the community. Success is pleasant when it comes after a life of accomplishment and achievement, so we should magnify the importance and pleasure of each future accomplishment.

Albert E. N. Gray says that successful people are influenced most by the desire for pleasing methods. Loafing, going to the movies, and sleeping late may all be pleasant methods, but the result of having no money is unpleasant. Doing those things that failures don't want to do may seem to have some disadvantages, but the resulting success is very pleasant. If the end or objective is to be pleasant, then the method must include planning, industry, enthusiasm, will power, and determination.

One of the great differences between success and failure is that the successful person focuses on the objective, whereas the unsuccessful person focuses on the present and sees nothing of great importance in the future. The unsuccessful person sees only obstacles in his opportunities, while the successful one sees opportunities in his obstacles.

The temporary upsets of the present can't hurt us much if our attention is fixed on the distant objective. For example, suppose that you have a long, hard tramp through the snow on a cold, stormy night. If you labor with no idea of the end and think only of the present cold, you are unhappy; but if you visualize the end and know that at the end of the journey there is a hot dinner, dry clothing, a warm fire, congenial friends, and a rich reward for your effort, that is an entirely different matter. The mental image of future warmth tends to overcome the present cold. To concentrate your thoughts on the dinner and the reward is far better psychology and good sense than to spend your strength thinking about how cold and disagreeable the weather is.

All of the joys and appetites are located in the imagination. If we keep our imagination focused on the objective, we have power. If we concentrate on the obstacle, we have discouragement. In one case we have motive and ambition; in the other, despair.

Napoleon once said, "I see only the objective. The obstacle must give way." Napoleon won his battles in his head before he won them on the field. He saw only the objective, and everything else was nothing. In the plentitude of his resources, every obstacle seemed to vanish. "There shall be no Alps," he said, and he built roads that climbed by gradation along the steepest precipices until Italy was within easy reach. Again and again he said to his men, "Beyond the Alps lies Italy," and in their minds they prelived all the delights they believed were in store for them at the end of the journey.

What a force was coiled up in the skull of Napoleon! He knew his business. He asked counsel of no one. He never blundered into success. He believed in Napoleon. His favorite rhetoric lay in his allusion to his star, and he styled himself the child of destiny. He risked everything; he spared nothing—neither ammunition nor money nor troops nor generals nor himself. That is the power created by a great imagination focused on its destiny. Napoleon was not a *good* man, but he had a powerful personality with immense capacities for sustained concentration. Someone called him "Organized Victory." He focused and pointed his life. He achieved centrality in his purpose. Psychologically speaking, he was all in one piece. Certainly before he started any undertaking, he knew where he was going.

We ought to practice regularly this kind of one-directional concentration with a clear-cut objective. This law of the objective has so many applications. We meet it in almost every act of life.

Some time ago, I attended a funeral at which, just before the funeral service and while the heirs were all present, the will of the deceased man was read. He had not visualized this hour when he wrote his will; when he wrote it, he was thinking of the present, not the hour preceding his funeral. He did not foresee that when his will was read he would not be there to explain and make adjustments. Had his imagination run ahead and lived this funeral hour before he wrote the will, he might have saved a lot of heartbreak, and the attitude of his family at the funeral would have been much more kindly toward him and themselves. I learned then that a person can have a public relations problem even after his death.

The imagination is a pretty handy apparatus. We need to let it run ahead and get the spirit and the lay of the land of the future and then come back and report before we make our plans. We shouldn't trust our perspective, because unaided it will deceive us by subtracting the importance from the future. This deception of perspective made Esau think that a mess of pottage today was more important than the birthright of the future.

We need to learn the art of living with our objective so that we can understand it before the time of our actual arrival; to make it as enticing as possible; to light it up so that it stands out like a great beacon. When we turn our thoughts to an objective, we raise up its image in our fancy, so we need to make that image of heroic size.

Gradually in our minds we can build our objective magnet stronger and stronger until success is easy and, like Gertrude Ederle, we may accomplish objectives that never before have been considered possible.

37 The Law of POSITIVE STATEMENT

Everyone interested in human relations should read again and again the autobiography of Benjamin Franklin. Many people think that for all-round excellence, Benjamin Franklin was the wisest man America has ever produced.

Franklin states in his autobiography the techniques he used to accomplish this position of real distinction. He records that he always carried with him a list of virtues he wanted to cultivate and a list of the vices in his personality which he wished to eliminate. He recalls that at one time in his life he was overbearing, sometimes approaching insolence. Fortunately one of his good friends talked with him about it, and, unlike most of us, Franklin was wise enough to listen to a recital of his own shortcomings without getting angry. Commenting about this, Franklin said:

> I made it a rule to forbear all direct contradiction to the sentiments of others, and all positive assertion of my own. I even forbid myself . . . the use of every word or expression that imported a fix'd opinion, such as *certainly, undoubtedly,* etc., and I adopted, instead of them, *I conceive, I apprehend,* or *I imagine* a thing to be so or so; or *it so appears to me at present.* When another asserted something I thought an error, I deny'd myself the pleasure of contradicting him abruptly, and of showing immediately some absurdity in his proposition; and in answering I began by observing that in certain cases or circumstances his opinion would be right, but in the present case there *appear'd* or *seem'd* to me some difference, etc. I soon found the advantage of this change in my manner; the conversations I engag'd in went on more pleasantly. The modest way in which I propos'd my opinions

> procur'd them a readier reception and less contradiction; I had less mortification when I was found to be in the wrong, and I more easily prevail'd with others to give up their mistakes and join with me when I happened to be in the right.

Mr. Franklin said that next only to character and integrity, this non-dogmatical attitude was of more help to him than any other one single thing.

A positive dogmatic statement often seems to set in motion the very forces that have tended to overcome it. A person who makes such a statement is immediately challenged by many people who otherwise would have found no fault in him. That is an easy way to get into an argument or a fight. No one is more offensive than a dogmatic, cocksure person who makes positive, arbitrary, unbending, and frequently untrue statements. It is much easier to ask a question and make a suggestion or cite the experience of someone else. You might even give him a hidden challenge. For example, a real estate salesman might say, "Do you think this home costs more than you are able to handle?" Then watch the customer straighten his shoulders and arise to meet the situation; if a dogmatic statement is made that he can easily pay such an amount, however, he may immediately begin to argue.

One such man is a teacher who is impressed that he should and does know all of the answers. As a result, he antagonizes his students even when he is right. Other people are so petty and so seemingly unpleasant in their positiveness that they develop in their hearers a horror of holding their opinions. Some people will believe an opposite thing only because they don't want to hold a common belief with someone who repels them. The overbearing attitude of a parent often will produce a revolt in the heart of a child, and a domineering husband may destroy the love of his wife. Many overzealous religious leaders have accomplished exactly opposite the effect they were attempting to achieve because of overpositiveness, and many sales have been lost by the same process. Things urged too hard often become repellent.

A great judge of human relations once said, "He that exalteth himself shall be abased, but he that humbleth himself shall be exalted." He understood the law that if a person took the position of "exalting himself in the spirit of dogmatic aggression, he would probably start in motion an opposition of forces which would be his undoing." If one wants to really exalt himself, he will follow the counsel of Benjamin Franklin and of Jesus Christ and beware of that kind of positiveness which can be so highly offensive.

Certainly there is a time when firmness and positiveness should be used, but it should be well seasoned with humility and sincere consideration for the feelings and opinions and judgment of other people. This does not mean one should deprecate oneself unduly or fish for compliments, for that is as vain as to exalt oneself. Always remember that a positive, dogmatic statement usually sets off a chain of negative reactions, whereas a qualified, well-considered statement will usually produce a positive reaction.

38 The Law of PROBABILITY

Successful living is the artistic application of a number of sciences. One of these has to do with the measurement of the effects of given causes. It is probable that in success, as in all other sciences, a given idea, given in a prescribed way, will result in a given answer, and if all the facts were known, the results of all of these could be predicted in advance.

Potential information comes under the heading of the law of probability. It is the law of averages. It is the law of expectancy. An understanding of the law of probability is important to us in every field because it is then possible to know in advance what we can do to change results to best serve us.

If one flips a coin into the air once, he may have no idea of whether it will fall a head or a tail. But if it is thrown into the air a thousand times, the law of probability will tell him with almost absolute certainty what the result will be: There will be an average of 500 heads and 500 tails. By this same law, it is possible to predict the outcome of many events in advance. We know approximately how many marriages there will be next year, as well as how many divorces. We can predict how many people will be killed on our highways in any given period.

The law of averages is the foundation on which the entire actuarial side of the insurance business is built. We know about how many people will die this year. We know what their ages will be and what will cause their deaths.

About the only thing we do not know about them is their names. According to the law of averages, we can also predict the length of people's life expectancy. This life expectancy can be changed by changing the circumstances that cause it.

In Jerusalem two thousand years ago, the average life expectancy at birth was nineteen years. In George Washington's day in America it was thirty-five years. When I was born it was forty-eight years. And in our present day of medical miracles and wonder drugs the little baby born in an American hospital this morning has an average expectation of life of seventy-two years.

This law of averages is also the science upon which the life insurance salesman himself operates. We know how much life insurance will be sold in the coming year and what kinds of policies the people will buy. We can tell in advance the effectiveness of selling by mail, or the power of human interest stories, or the results of a given prospecting system. We can tell in advance, on the average, exactly how many people will react favorably to any given stimulation. It is possible to predict how many interviews it will take to get one sale, how many people will not keep their appointments, etc. This law says that one particular agent must get six no's in order to get one yes, while another salesman who is more effectively prepared will need only two no's in order to get the desired yes.

Studying the facts enables us to determine why one agent gets a bigger percentage of yesses than another, and we are able to chart our work with an intelligent concept of exactly what to expect. By being able to tell in advance what is going to happen and why it happens, we are able to intercede in our own behalf to change our averages upward. With an effective knowledge of the law of averages, we may develop effective salesmanship so we know exactly where our problems lie and what should be done about them.

This principle is true in other fields. People engaged in missionary work should understand the powerful law of probability. Conversion takes place when certain conditions are produced in the mind and heart of the convert. One set of procedures for discovering investigators, securing interviews, and making the presentation may give one a .250

percentage, whereas another set of procedures may raise his score and increase his success many times.

Through effective record keeping, so that we know what the facts are and what makes us successful and what makes us unsuccessful, we can eliminate the ineffective and concentrate on those procedures that have a proven success record, and thus we can increase our effectiveness many times. If we keep accurate accounts of our work and learn to effectively measure and evaluate our efforts, we can lift our success to any desired level. This is the essence of progress.

We can also learn what causes failure and how to eliminate it from our program. For example, we know that discouragement always tends to destroy our success. In making the most of our lives we cannot afford many periods of negative thinking, idleness, sin, or depression. If the worth of our souls is greater than the value of the earth, then each indulgence in drunkenness, immorality, sloth, or other disobedience costs us a tremendous total.

One of the problems that usually confronts a salesman is that he does not understand the actual value of time or what each prospect or each interview is worth in actual commission dollars. When he becomes negative and discouraged, he thinks no one will buy anyway, and so he doesn't work. If he knew his law of averages, he would know that every hour and every prospect and every interview has a definite cash value. He would also be aware that for every discouragement and every negative thought he is losing a definite amount of money.

And so it is with our eternal exaltation. Eternal damnation itself is made up of so many individual wrong thoughts, sins, and failures. If we could place a value of a trillion dollars on our eternal exaltation and then if we lost it by a thousand evil acts, the law of averages would say that each individual evil act had a price tag on it of a billion dollars.

I have a personal problem of passing by the pie counter at the cafeteria without an indulgence that causes me damage because it increases my overweight and acts as a liability on my health. One of the difficulties is that the price tag on the pie says that it only costs fifty cents, and that always seems to me to be too great a bargain to pass up. But if the price of pie went up to five hundred dollars per piece, my appetite for pie would be completely destroyed. And if the price of pie went up to five thousand dollars a piece, then no one could force me to ever consider eating pie.

We have this same kind of problem in trying to live successfully. If a person wants to have fun, he might say, "Let's go and get drunk, or get high on dope, or be immoral." Of course none of such people are happy. But in addition, if we understood that every evil act has a price tag, our attitudes would be completely different.

I know of a young woman who had a moral problem. She was cautioned against any repetition of her evil. Then when she discovered that she was going to be an unwed mother, she quit her job and moved to another state to have her baby. After the baby was born, she put it up for adoption. Eventually she returned home and got her job back, but during her absence she had lost $12,000 in actual income. But even worse, she had also lost a lot of self-respect; she had cost her parents a great deal of humiliation and unhappiness; and she had displeased God. If she had been on speaking terms with the law of probability, even though she was lacking in moral responsibility, she would have been impressed with the price she would certainly be asked to pay for each immoral sin that she committed. And the same law applies either negatively or positively to everything that we do.

Knowledge of the law of averages as it applies to each of us can teach us how to more effectively overcome each problem and produce those attitudes that will give us a higher percentage of successes by turning our defeats into triumphs. By this process, we can greatly increase the probability of our own success.

Every missionary knows that an increase in the quality of his investigators quickly raises the percentage of conversions, and when he increases the number of his investigators his number of successes is again increased proportionally. That is, when a missionary doubles the number of his discussions, he not only doubles his exposure, but he also doubles his practice and may therefore quadruple the result.

The law of probability can be a powerful instrument in the hands of anyone who works with people or events, providing it is followed scientifically. Planning, record keeping, and good judgment are so closely related that they cannot be considered separately. One's judgment is never any better than his information, and we must know what causes success before we can produce it.

39 The Law of REASON

The other day I received a letter from a seventeen-year-old student who indicated that she was always frightened when in her classes or other places she attempted to speak before groups of people. She explained to me that Satan knew of her weakness and was capitalizing on it in every possible way to embarrass and humiliate her and keep her from success. She wanted me to explain to her how she could thwart Satan, overcome her fear, and develop ability in speaking in public.

Such a question may seem a bit elementary to some; yet some form of this question of how to do things perplexes almost everyone, and we frequently prevent our own accomplishment by blaming our weaknesses on some other person or circumstance. I tried to explain to this fine young woman that God never forces anyone to do right and Satan has no power to force anyone to do wrong. Someone has said that God always votes for us and Satan always votes against us and then they ask us to vote to break the tie. It is how we vote that gives our lives significance and value.

Most people who fail probably fail because they have never taken time to learn how to succeed. Many people who would like to be great athletes or artists or doctors or lawyers or salesmen or just great human beings fall down because they don't know how to achieve their desires. One person may have in his mind as good an understanding of basketball as anyone who has ever lived in the world, but he will never succeed as a basketball player until he gets out on the court and, through months and years of rehearsal and drill, develops the required skills of a champion.

The prospective basketball player who doesn't spend a lot of time in practice and drill might be compared to the student who was asked by the teacher to define vacuum. The student replied, "I have it in my head but I can't express it." We have every potential skill within us, and we must learn to get it out. Everyone has a vein of greatness, but he must learn to command the shaft by which he may draw out the gold.

The greatest responsibility that God has ever laid upon the shoulders of any human being is to make the best and the most of his own life, and we must take upon ourselves the obligation for our own training and supervision. While it is true that a male child born with one leg may not have the same prospects for being a champion football quarterback as someone born with two legs, yet that handicap may be of special help to him in some other direction. God created us in his own image and has endowed us with a set of his attributes and potentialities. Certainly no two human beings have potentialities and abilities that exactly match each other, yet God has endowed each one of us with the miraculous power to reason as an incomparable aid in making the most of ourselves.

The dictionary defines reason as that quality of sense and understanding which is the guiding and directing faculty of the mind. Sound judgment gives clear comprehension, especially in practical affairs. It is based on understanding of basic general principles or laws or warranted presumptions that support logical conclusions, explain facts, and validate and point out a right course of conduct. Good judgment is the ability to trace out the implication in a combination of facts, suppositions, and intellect. Logical reasoning gives us clear insight. When we abandon reason and make decisions based on signs, omens, or superstitions, we sometimes cause more problems instead of eliminating those that we already have. When we blame the devil or our parents or our circumstances, we may also cause problems.

A fine woman and her splendid husband recently came to discuss one of their problems. They wanted to know why the Lord had never permitted them to have any children. They stated that they had kept the commandments and paid their tithing, attended church, and served in the Church. The assumption was that they must have offended the Lord in some way, and so he was punishing them. I do not know all the reasons why things happen to people, but I do know that some of the worst criminals and some of the most imbecilic and most physically inferior people can have children. It seems that these facts should have suggested to their reasoning power that unworthiness was not the cause of their childlessness.

One of the important ways to develop logic, judgment, and reason is to be conscious of poor judgment and lack of reason as it manifests itself in ourselves and in others. On one occasion four fine young men were going to a football game. There was no violation of traffic laws or liquor laws, but there was an accident, and one of the four was killed. The father of the deceased young man was, of course, heartbroken. The driver of the car was not killed, and the father of the deceased young man later heard the father of the driver explain his son's survival on the grounds of his supposed faithfulness and the consequent love and protection that God had for him. The clear inference was that the boy who was killed was not faithful. This was very disturbing to the father whose son had been killed.

If we were completely familiar with all the facts concerning death and accidents, we would have to explain this kind of a death on some other basis. It is not always the worst people who die nor the best people who live. Neither is it always the best people who are the most successful. God makes his sun to shine on the evil and the good, and he sends his rain on the just and the unjust. One thing that he has tried to make very clear is that he does not balance his books every Saturday night. The final judgment has been reserved for that time when all of the accounts have been audited and handed in.

Many people run their lives by how they feel at the moment instead of basing their actions and decisions on more logical assumptions. Many even abandon the word of the Lord himself in order to satisfy their own feelings and emotions.

Over the years many have used omens, signs, suspicions, or hopes to replace reason as a basis for their conduct. In Jesus' day the people asked him to give them a sign, and his reply was that a wicked and adulterous generation seeks after a sign. Yet even in our day we go too much by signs that do not mean what we see, want, and think them to mean.

A young man was once trying to decide whether or not he should go into the ministry or remain on the farm. Then one day he saw two great letters in the clouds in the sky. There was what appeared to be a large "P" and a large "C." The young man felt that this was his answer and that the Lord had said to him "preach Christ." However, his father's interpretation was that the sign said to "plant corn."

Many people are influenced by the belief that God is picking on them and punishing them for some real or imaginary sin. They feel that they were born wrong and that there is no hope. Probably the most widespread disease in the world is an inferiority complex. God has given us one of the fundamental principles when he said, "Many are called but few are chosen." (D&C 121:40.) Most people probably fail in being chosen because they have not chosen themselves nor adopted logical procedures that would guarantee their success. Rather, they have elected to follow their emotions instead of their brains; then they feel inferior and sorry for themselves, and believe that there is no hope.

God has given to almost every person ever born possibilities and potentialities many times greater than anyone ever lives up to. The surest way to any accomplishment is to live by the word of the Lord, for he has said that we may have any blessing that we desire if we are willing to obey the law upon which that blessing is predicated.

40 The Law of SELF-CONTROL

One of the most recent engineering marvels of our age is power steering, by the aid of which a 300-horsepower engine in a car of several thousand pounds traveling at tremendous speed may be controlled by the pressure of one finger. Engineering science, through brakes, steering devices, and other inventions, has given man fingertip control over the most powerful of engines.

If someone would like to gain everlasting fame, he could do it by perfecting a device whereby a man could get a comparable degree of control over himself.

A man usually has great authority over his limbs. If he wills that his finger bend, it will obey. His legs move merely at the suggestion of his will. It's wonderful to contemplate mental power with authority over physical substances. This authority has different degrees of control. A man has rather complete control over his fingers but little or no control over his heart or liver. If one wills that his eyes close, they respond, but if he wills that his heart stop, it pays no attention. Between these two extremes lies all the rest of our self-control. One has great authority over his feet, not quite so much over his tongue, and, in diminishing order, his ideas, his industry, his feelings, his emotions, his instincts.

The dictionary says that to control is to exercise a directioning, restraining, or governing influence. Self-control would, therefore, mean to exercise direction, restraint, motivation, and government over our organs, our faculties, our emotions, and our personalities; and the ultimate in self-control would be to obtain a sort of fingertip power-steering arrangement so that all of our faculties and inclinations would respond to our slightest touch. Then our personalities or ideas would never run wild nor would our emotions get out of control.

We should not be too discouraged if this jurisdiction is not complete at first. All living things at their birth are small and misshapen. Even ideas are not usually born fully symmetrical, wellformed, with maximum power and polish. That is a matter of subsequent growth and development. One of the great purposes of training is to increase our authority over our component parts.

Try to think of anything in the world that would be more important than one little gadget that would spell out self-control for us. It would include in it all of the following:

Self-inquiry
Self-analysis
Self-criticism
Self-correction
Self-knowledge
Self-instruction
Self-motivation
Self-improvement
Self-reliance
Self-control

The greatest accomplishment is to train the mind to extend and increase its authority over the body. The business of living is probably one of the best places to teach ourselves self-control. Life is also the place where we are most highly rewarded for the development of self-mastery.

One of the first steps toward self-control is planning. We know something about what we must do, and we also should understand our own resources and shortcomings. Then once every day we should sit down and plan and think and analyze and reason. This is where we make a program for the activities of the day, but it is also where we make decisions and build morale for ourselves and decide on our projected improvements and our goals. The work that one does above and beyond his objective is highly stimulating. It is helpful to the personality to feel that we are going beyond the expected, that we are making a superior effort.

Checkup and follow-up are important. We should never give anyone an assignment and then fail to check up. It's even more dangerous with ourselves, for we should develop the very best ways to motivate, restrain, and guide ourselves.

In our work every day, we should watch and practice our control—time control, idea control, enthusiasm control, industry control, accomplishment control, and so forth. This is one way to become a great doctor or a great lawyer or a great salesman or a great human being. Self-control is the most effective means to any kind of success, power, and happiness.

41 The Law of SELF-DECEPTION

Since I was a child, I have heard that the ostrich buries his head in the sand when he is afraid, to hide from the danger that threatens him. I have asked several people who should know something about ostriches, and I am convinced that ostriches do not do this. Someone has maligned the poor bird by assigning to him a trait characteristic of certain human beings but not of ostriches. When an ostrich is frightened, he either fights or runs.

However, think how this characteristic of trying to hide from our fears manifests itself in some people. In the movies when a woman is terribly frightened, she usually screams and covers her eyes with her hands so that she cannot see the horror or danger by which she is threatened. When a person is operated on, he closes his eyes so he cannot see himself get hurt. When we see a terrible accident, we turn our faces away so we cannot see it. To most unpleasant sights we close our eyes. When we smell something unpleasant, we hold our noses. When we hear something unpleasant, we put our fingers in our ears. When we think something unpleasant, we take a dose of sleeping pills or tranquilizers.

This trait of hiding from disagreeable facts is especially manifest when someone is trying to make suggestions to help us. It is a paradox that the recipients of advice should feel no annoyance when they ought to feel it and yet feel so much when they ought not to. They are usually vexed not at all at having committed the fault, but very angry at being reproved for it. On the contrary, they ought to feel grieved at the crime and glad for the correction.

One of the things that often holds us back in our success is the deliberate attempt we make to hide from the facts when the facts are unpleasant. Advice is seldom valued, though there is a great deal of advising and very little listening. Usually we do not want advice; we want flattery. And yet one cannot easily be our flatterer and our friend at the same time. Some people actually owe more to bitter enemies than to pleasant friends. The former sometimes speak the truth; the latter seldom do. An enemy is often a friend in disguise who stings us into action. He tells us the truth about ourselves. Cato asserted that wise men profit more from fools than fools do from wise men, for some wise men try to avoid the faults of fools, but fools seldom try to imitate the good examples of wise men.

There is a great book entitled *Damaged Souls,* written by Gamaliel Bradford, which is a series of biographies of near-great men who were prevented from becoming what their virtues intended because they also had accompanying faults. The author said that there was no evidence that any one of the men ever developed the ability to stand off and look critically at himself.

Some mental patients never look into themselves, into their way of living and thinking, in an effort to see whether their symptoms may be associated with their ways of living. The reason why they do not is obvious. They are not going to see what they do not want to see; they cannot be expected to destroy their defenses, and so many of these unfortunates are not even aware of their troubles.

Each human being is trusted with the responsibility of making an effective personality. Our judgment is no better than our information, and when we deliberately practice self-deception, our judgment becomes useless or actually harmful. Kings and other rulers are often particularly unfortunate. They are shut off and shielded from the truth on every side. They get their facts secondhand and are lied to all day long. Consequently they become in time incapable of digesting truth.

Most people have an epidermis that is too thin to stand criticism. What we usually want is salve—soft, pleasant, emolient, gracious salve. We demand praise, not suggestion. We wish to be saved from the mischief of our vices, not from the vices themselves. The Jews said to Moses, "Tell us pleasant things and we will hearken unto you," as if the agreeableness of the thing should regulate their belief. But most of us are like that.

Someone said, "Truly, it is an evil thing to be full of faults, but it is still a greater evil to be full of them and be unwilling to recognize them, since that is to add the further fault of voluntary delusion." If you would escape vexation, reprove yourself liberally and others sparingly. We do not like others to deceive us. We do not think it fair that they should be held in higher esteem by us than they deserve. Neither is it fair that we should deceive them and wish them to esteem us more highly than we deserve. But good or bad, almost the last thing anyone wants is counsel.

No criminal ever calls himself a criminal. Jesse James thought himself a benefactor to society. Napoleon said, "I believe I will be without parallel in history, that a plain man shall have attained to such amazing power without committing a single crime." All this, of course, is self-deception. It is a crime to deceive other people, and it is a calamity to deceive ourselves, especially when we go so far that it is often impossible to get ourselves undeceived.

If you really wish to improve yourself, you need someone on the sidelines to coach you and to observe your mistakes and warn you against repetition. Without someone to tell you the truth about your annoying mannerisms and bad habits and inexcusable mistakes, you may fall into the pit of self-delusion where disaster lurks. Thus, for self-improvement, get a close friend to tell you off occasionally. He will act as a mirror in which you can see yourself as others see you.

Criticism is the hardest medicine to take, but it keeps us awake, while the kindness of a courteous friend is an opiate that puts us to sleep. The "yes man" seldom gives any constructive help. This is an area where even an enemy might be helpful, because he may be vulgar enough and merciless enough to say the things about us that will enable us to rid ourselves of our most serious shortcomings. The wise person always throws himself on the side of his assailants, for it is more in his interest than it is in theirs to find out his weak points. And, of course, a wise person will listen instead of fighting back. This inability to learn the truth about ourselves is a stumbling block on which we often fall and break the necks of our personalities and our success.

To think clearly, a person must arrange for regular periods of solitude when he can concentrate and indulge his imagination without distraction. As a rule we may become successful by the application of the same principles other successful people use. While principles are easily available to all of us, we sometimes envy others their wealth without ever thinking of studying their philosophy and appropriating it to our own use. We look at a successful person in the hour of his triumph and think of him as a "born" success, but we overlook the importance of analyzing his methods, and we forget the price he had to pay and is paying in careful, well-organized preparation.

Each of us should at least be aware of the tendency within us to hide from the facts, and every effective person should develop the ability to look within himself.

One of the medical sciences is called vivisection, by which a doctor cuts into living tissues—not to kill, but to study the workings of vital organs so he can find out and cure the hidden trouble. A kind of vivisection—or mental introspection—for ourselves is just as important, and if we do not master the process by practice, it may be just about as painful. That is, it may hurt some people just as much to cut into their personalities as to cut into their abdomens.

Everyone ought to have an employer or a marriage partner or a religious counselor or a trusted friend who can cut into the tissues of his attitudes and habits occasionally, not to kill him but to bring him back to life. It's easy to see faults from the sidelines, but everyone has a blind spot where he himself is concerned. If we are so fortunate as to have someone who will occasionally give us the facts about our problems, we shouldn't get angry at him. We should listen and keep our heads out of the sand and our eyes and ears open.

We should never deceive our friends, but even more important, we should not deceive ourselves.

42 The Law of SELF-PITY

The human personality is the most perfect piece of machinery ever known. Under the best circumstances it can stand up under all kinds of adversity, mistreatment, and loss of health and still say, as did Henley in his "Invictus," written after he had become a hopeless cripple, "I am the master of my fate; I am the captain of my soul."

However, like all other machinery, the human personality sometimes gets out of order. It's pretty difficult to break down a man's morale or prevent his progress as long as he remains sound at the core. The breakdown doesn't come until a weakening process starts to take place within. The greatest ocean can't sink the smallest ship until some of the water gets inside; and so long as we can keep our personality machinery in an airtight, waterproof compartment, nothing can hurt us.

Adversity and problems may actually serve to strengthen us. When a group of people feel the same weight of trouble, they are usually drawn together and they demonstrate what a superb thing a human being can be when under great stress. Then they are often willing to make great sacrifices and show the tremendous power of cooperation. But sometimes, if we feel that adversity strikes harder at us than at others and that there is some injustice, our emotional stress skyrockets and there tends to be a breakdown of our machinery on the inside.

It is interesting that in all of life, no one can hurt us but ourselves, and probably the greatest hazard to the harmonious operation of the human machine is the insidious thing that happens when, for some real or imaginary reason, a person begins to feel sorry for himself. More often than not the reason for the disease that we call self-pity is imagined rather than real, for self-pity is not confined to the poor or sick or unfortunate. The issues are often greatly magnified or purely imaginary.

Pity for others is a feeling of grief or pain aroused by weakness, misfortune, or distress. It does not usually arise where there is a feeling of equality; we usually pity those who are less fortunate than we. Pity implies weakness. This kind of pity may be offensive but it is harmless; the really malignant kind of pity is self-pity. God can forgive us our sins, but who can forgive us our despair?

Self-pity is a feeling of real or imagined unworthiness, an inferiority complex without hope, an allergy to ourselves. Self-pity is pathetic; it is weakness. It has some symptoms in common with extreme battle fatigue, in which one has no heart to continue the fight. It is often born out of paying too much attention to the things one lacks rather than being grateful for what he has, or it might originate at any one of several other sources:

1. An effective personality needs to be fed by accomplishment, and when one indulges too liberally in laziness or bad habits, there is no food left in the imagination.

2. We make unfavorable comparisons with others. We imagine that life can cheat us.

3. Our thinking becomes crooked. We start looking at ourselves as into a trick mirror, which shows us and our condition distorted and deformed. We begin calling things by the wrong names.

The cure is usually the reverse of the cause. Like everything else, the most important cure is prevention:

1. We should summon all of our energy to feed our personalities with accomplishment so there will be an honest basis for self-respect.

2. We ought not to let our feelings or our imaginations or our daydreams run away with our reason and our judgment. We must learn to think straight.

3. We should get in the habit of thinking about what we have as well as what we lack. Comparisons with others who are far ahead of us are good if kept on a healthy, balanced basis, but when we see these through a distorted imagination, we see a wrong point of view.

The following questions are good for a distorted imagination that is centered in self-pity. Think about them.

1. Where would you rather live than where you presently live? (Many people who express dissatisfaction with their circumstances are really much better off than are people in so many oppressed areas of the world.)

2. When would you rather have lived than right now? Most people have lived in either prehistoric or ancient times without all of the advantages of present-day civilization. How would you like to have lived in the dark ages?

3. Who would you rather be than who you are? Can you think of even one person you would change places with?

4. What work would you rather do than what you are doing? Many people in the occupations around you have far less opportunity than you. If you can think of one occupation you would like better, you can easily change, for this is a free country, and opportunities surround us on every side.

Everyone should beware of self-pity. It is an internal sore by which the personality is immobilized, but it can be cured by the right thoughts and a little appropriate accomplishment. Most people are less fortunate than are we. This should console us. Even if we are oppressed by anxiety, that anxiety will not last if we take appropriate measures against it. Life cannot cheat us, and no one can harm us but ourselves.

43 The Law of SELF-SUPERVISION

One of the curiosities of the human personality is that only a relatively few people ever learn to direct their own efforts according to their own previously thought-out plans. Many experiments have shown that if you have a five-man job to be done, it can be accomplished more quickly if you make one person the boss and hold him responsible for keeping the other four busy.

The amount of supervision required largely determines what a person is worth. If he requires a lot of supervision, he gets one amount; if he requires a little less supervision, he gets a little larger income; and when he can be depended upon to do his job without any supervision, he is worth still more. Of course, at the top of the list is the person who does his own work, on his own initiative, following his own plans which he himself has drawn and initiated, and who in addition stimulates others. He is the one who receives the top income.

The tremendous expense involved in supervision is one of the heaviest burdens borne by our civilization. It is one of the great wastes in government, in church work, and in business affairs. Too often the initiative, the motivation, the reminding, the pep talks, and the planning must be provided for those who are unable to do those things for themselves. An interesting set of figures was recently released by the United States government that indicates this shortcoming in people. People are generally divided into three groups as follows:

2 percent: Work, manage, plan
14 percent: Work, manage
84 percent: Work

No matter what the job to be done may be, most people can learn how to do the actual work involved. Take, for example, the job of a farmer. Most normal persons can learn to plow, plant, cultivate, irrigate, and fertilize. Yet only a few ever become successful farmers. Why? Eighty-four percent can do the work all right, but that's all they can do. When the boss leaves, they sit down. They never learn to manage themselves and operate under their own supervision. Fourteen percent can do the work, and they can also manage themselves. When the supervisor is not present, these workers, unlike the 84 percent, do not quit. They keep going whether the boss is present or not. They not only do more work but also save the cost of their own supervision. In addition, someone must plan their work for them—the 2 percent at the top. They can work, they can manage themselves, and they can also plan.

It is fine to be able to do important work skillfully and properly. And yet that is probably the smallest part of success. There are probably few salesmen, for example, who could not easily double their sales. They could easily learn all of the steps involved in planning, prospecting, preapproach, direct mail, approach, interviewing, answering objections, closing the sale, and so forth. It isn't the work that bothers us; it's learning to supervise and motivate ourselves—to think, to organize, and to execute our plans on our own power.

Most people, if left to their own devices, either sit down or lie down or fall down on the job. The executive part of their personalities is nonproductive. The initiative and ability to keep going seem to have been ironed out of their personalities, and the planning ability has dried up in their minds.

This is a quality of partial nonproductiveness that is seen in nature. For example, Bing and Lambert cherry trees are incapable of producing fruit if left by themselves. They have no fertilizing pollen, and so a pollinator must be planted among them. Then the wind and the bees carry the pollen to those trees that are incapable of self-fertilization.

Many people are like that with regard to their work. One might be an excellent workman but not a self-starter. His initiative, ability to supervise, and ability to plan remain unproductive. Even though the necessary supervision is costly, such a worker must pay the heavy price and have someone stand over him and keep him going.

Elbert Hubbard was thinking about this situation when he said, "I am looking out through the library window into the apple orchard, and I see millions of blossoms that will never materialize and become fruit for lack of vitalization." The destiny of an apple blossom is that it should become an apple, and the destiny of a human soul is that it may become even as God. But neither of these things happens unless that vitalizing element is introduced that makes us productive.

The highest classification of effort is exerted by the person who can work on his own power and who can also motivate others. He usually determines his own pay.

In the process of training ourselves for success, we mustn't forget the importance of learning to stand on our own feet without always having to have someone there to prop us up, supply our ideas, and motivate us. One may be an excellent salesman, but if he doesn't know how to organize his time and is not capable of continuous effort on his own power, he allows this deficiency to iron the zeal out of his mind and immobilize his ambition until he becomes comparatively nonproductive.

There are many advantages in learning self-supervision, including the following:

1. Our pay is increased.

2. We get the kind of supervision we like best, which is our own. The best motivation always comes from the inside. When we have to have others supervise us, we often get someone whose personality does not harmonize with ours. If he is the supervisor, we must follow his ideas rather than our own. Frequently we do our work grudgingly because we resent our supervisor.

3. Many people in many kinds of work are not able to manage themselves, but instead of buckling in and learning

how to discipline themselves, they quit their jobs and go to work for someone else. The newness of the supervision satisfies them for a while, but it isn't long before they again feel the temptation to jump to something else.

4. One of the most thrilling things in the world is to work for ourselves, to plan our own work, develop our own ideas, and be our own persons. This is also the way to growth and happiness.

Success lies largely in the ability to handle ourselves. One of the most exalting feelings one will ever know is the feeling that he is bigger than circumstances and that he can stand on his own feet and make his own way against all obstacles. We reach this point by learning something that most people never find out: the art of self-supervision. Then we are bigger than anything that can happen to us.

44 The Law of the SPLIT PERSONALITY

In recent years we have heard a great deal about the splitting of the atom. We know the results of splits in political parties, business organizations, and families, and of other situations in which people become divided against one another.

A split in the personality is where a man is divided against himself. Psychiatrists technically describe this situation as schizophrenia. The personality is divided so as to give the effect of two or more people. A famous fictional example is that of Dr. Jekyll and Mr. Hyde, in which, by means of a split personality, a kindly physician by day became a ruthless criminal by night.

To some degree each of us may suffer from this disorder. Each of us in varying degrees is two or more people. We develop inner conflicts that produce a multiple personality. Ambition urges one of us forward while inertia holds the other one back.

Psychiatrists can testify that many individuals make tragic and ofttimes futile efforts to achieve peace within themselves by compartmentalizing themselves. That is, in a subconscious effort to bring about harmony, they split up their personalities and house each in a tiny, soundproof compartment. By this process, they effect a spurious inner harmony by parceling out to competing philosophies the various phases of their own experience. All of the compartments are housed in one body but remain a veritable crowd of different compartmentalized selves, as much strangers to one another as are the residents of an urban apartment house.

Most of us know how to become great human beings—most of us want to be great human beings—but we lack the ability to integrate our deeds with our creeds. We believe in honesty with all our hearts in one compartment, but we take advantage of someone in the other compartment if it will bring us an advantage. We can get new ideas in great abundance in our idea compartment, but we fail to follow through. A dreamer is strong in one place and weak in another.

If we could learn to tightly tie our personalities together so we could move with absolute unity and power, most of our troubles would be over. Then to think would be to act; to believe would be to perform; to know would be to do and to be. The discord between creed and deed has been at the root of innumerable wrongs throughout civilization. It is the weakness of political parties, churches, states, associations, and persons. It gives both institutions and men split personalities.

When we accept an idea in principle and do not practice it, we drive the wedge a little deeper into the personality. People with split personalities do not emulate the successful people whom they read and think about. Our problem in success is to develop a personality that is all in one piece and that is pointed and concentrated. When any person can accomplish this feat of tying himself together, and can have a single, integrated personality instead of a compartmentalized personality, his success is assured.

One person who probably did this as well as anyone else was Mohandas K. Gandhi. When he was young, he had lots of problems. He regarded himself as a coward. He had a bad temper. He had many personality disadvantages. He lived in a dozen compartments, each going in a different direction, each with a different aim.

Then he decided to pull himself together. He began by putting himself under severe discipline. His mother taught him that to eat meat was wrong, inasmuch as it necessitated the destruction of life, so Gandhi pledged to his mother that he would remain a strict vegetarian throughout his life. After his mother's death some of his friends tried to persuade him that there was no life in unfertilized eggs, and therefore he could eat these without breaking his pledge; but Gandhi knew his mother's definition of meat, and inasmuch as he had made the pledge with her, her definition must remain binding.

Then Gandhi was taken very ill and his life was despaired of. His physicians tried to persuade him that if he would drink a little beef broth, his life might be saved, but Gandhi said, "Even for life itself we may not do certain things. There is only one course open to me—to die, but never to break my pledge."

That's what it would be like to be all in one piece. As a result of this trait of integrity, Gandhi's followers renamed him the Mahatma, or the Great Soul. Gandhi said, "How can I control others, if I cannot control myself?" Louis Fischer says that not since Socrates has the world seen Gandhi's equal for absolute self-control and composure. He didn't practice his belief just when it was in his interest.

Gandhi spent his life trying to free India from the British, and when the time came that the British were engaged in the Battle of Britain and could not even spare one soldier for the defense of India, Gandhi's friends decided that now was the time to gain independence for their country. However, Gandhi had preached nonviolence; the ordinary compartmentalized personality might have forgotten his philosophy long enough to accept his freedom, but not Gandhi's. He said, "We will not steal even our freedom." His fellow citizens rose up against him, but he fought them down. He said, "No matter what happens, if everyone shall turn away leaving me to fight the battle alone, still I will never violate my pledge." Thus, he stood by the British until the Battle of Britain had been won, and then he renewed his peaceful negotiations for the freedom of India.

Gandhi accomplished for India without violence what Washington did for America through the Revolutionary

War. The people of India understood that Gandhi was absolutely honest, that he could be trusted whether the facts were working for or against his interests, and that his motives were right. He took ideas seriously, and when he accepted an idea in principle, he felt that not to practice it was dishonest.

We each ought to get ourselves organized, all in one piece, and under one command. We ought to make decisions about things and then stand on our decisions in every detail. If we decide to be honest, we should be honest all of the time, not just when we think we won't be discovered. We ought not to accept an assignment unless we are going to carry it out. When we plan a day's work, we ought to carry it through regardless of the inconvenience to ourselves. For every word we ought to put up a spiritual bond guaranteeing faithful performance.

We should stop trifling with success. An integrated personality means one understands that to think is to do; to promise is to perform. Faith should mean works, and desire should mean industry. In unity strength is applied to the personality as to no other thing. If "a house divided against itself cannot stand," how much less an individual! Let us each begin now—today—to work diligently at developing a personality that is unified. The law of the split personality is a law of negative value: let's work on making it a positive force for good in our lives.

45 The Law of SYMBOLS

The New York Yankees had just won the 1952 World Series in baseball by beating Brooklyn. Brooklyn had won the first game of the series, and then Mickey Mantle, Yankee center fielder, predicted on a radio program that the Yankees would win the series. He knew that every Yankee player carried inside his uniform the great tradition of championship. He told of the first time he himself had ever put on a Yankee uniform and the feeling of pride he felt in this great ball club. The Yankee uniform was a symbol of championship; it had been invested over the years with great tradition.

The Yankees won their first World Series in 1923, and in the twenty-nine years following they played in the series nineteen times and won it fifteen times. During that long period the faces changed and the names changed. There was no longer a Dimaggio or a Ruth or a Gehrig, but the uniform remained the same, and so did the result. It was said of the tired Yankee pitcher who pitched the last game of one World Series that he was throwing more with his heart than with his weary arm. When one puts his heart into the fight, things usually happen.

Even small boys, when they begin to play baseball, save their money to buy uniforms, because they know that one can play a better game if he is in uniform. That's an interesting psychological principle. When one puts on the uniform of the team, interesting things begin to happen. Not only do they look better on the outside, but what is more important, a change also takes place on the inside. When one puts on the uniform of the group, he stands for the group. He is no longer playing for himself; he is playing for the team. A player in uniform has a greater responsibility; he is more loyal; he has more pride in the outfit; he is more anxious to win; the honor of the team is at stake.

The dictionary says that a symbol is something that stands for something else; it is an emblem, a type, a character, a tradition, a confession of faith. But whatever it is, if it is properly enshrined, it gives us more than our natural power.

A few years ago when the government set out to create a military force, a lot of inexperienced young men were drafted from the office, the service station, the farm, the college, and other areas. These young men were to do the most important job in the world: preserve the world's freedom. The first thing the government did to transform these inexperienced young men into responsible military personnel was to put them in uniform. They were given certain insignia, rank, and assignments that included responsibility and authority.

Almost immediately young men who had previously been washing windshields and doing other ordinary jobs now became heroes, statesmen, and patriots. They flew flying fortresses, devised strategy, and dispensed justice. A great change took place almost overnight. The young soldier was no longer a common citizen; he had subscribed to and become a part of the great tradition of America that included the spirit of Valley Forge, Gettysburg. Chateau Thierry, and the Belgian Bulge. The welfare of his country was now in his hands, and he would discharge that responsibility with the same fidelity that had characterized other great patriots of America.

In life we live largely by symbols. The symbol may be a ring on the finger or a light in the window or a flag in the sky. It may be the uniform of one's country, the cloth of his church, the robe of the judiciary, or the emblem of his company that he wears on his coat or in his heart. But to the right person the right symbol may develop a spirit that is one of the finest attributes of success. It gives him additional power; it makes him greater than himself.

To what heights may a man ascend if he has behind him the force of a great cause and inside him the spirit of his office? What a thrilling picture to contemplate—a great cause represented by a man at his best!

Now think of situations in our daily lives. Elbert Hubbard once said that "business at its best is the process of ministering to human needs; therefore, business is essentially a divine calling." Each morning as we take hold of our share of the work of the world, we ought to think of it in that way and do it in that spirit. As workers we are also soldiers engaged in a peacetime war against poverty, ignorance, insecurity, and unhappiness, and our individual successes frequently depend upon the success of the team. Neither doctors nor employees nor teachers nor church workers live unto themselves alone. If the uniform of the New York Yankees can have such a positive effect on the hearts and accomplishments of individuals what could happen to us when we properly wear the uniform of our country or our business firm or our religious group? When a person gets into the church, many benefits accrue to him more or less automatically, but when the church gets into the person is when things really begin to happen.

When we go down into the waters of baptism we take upon ourselves certain obligations and make certain promises. Hands are lain upon our heads and we are confirmed members of the Church, and from those having authority we receive the gift of the Holy Ghost. When we are ordained to the priesthood, we put on the symbolic uniform that identifies us with its authority and its appropriate behavior. When we are called to serve as missionaries, we represent the Church and the Lord. We are asked to look like missionaries, dress like missionaries, and act like missionaries.

When we get married we go into the House of the Lord to organize the most important of all earthly institutions, the family. We dress in the robes of the priesthood. We make covenants of faithfulness, loyalty, and righteousness.

We make covenants not just merely for a week or a year—they are for eternity. And the one who lays his covenants aside is being false to his ideal, to his family, and to God.

Whether in politics or government, the work of the world or the work of the Lord, we all like to play on a winning team. We like to be proud of our outfit; we like to have confidence in our leaders. In each area of our lives, we should be fighting for a great cause, and we ought to have the spirit of righteousness and success. Then we become stronger than we were.

There is magic in spirit when one has the attitude of any great accomplishment; then weariness is not a problem. When Columbus discovered America, the natives told him of an herb that would take away fatigue. That herb is still growing here—but we should look for it in people and not in the ground. When one has the spirit of righteousness, the spirit of truth, the spirit of success, then he is not disturbed by the little difficulties that so often force a miscarriage in the enterprises of lesser persons. Dressed in the appropriate uniform to which he has made full commitment, his spirit grows tall and his fiber becomes tough enough to endure any assault that is made upon it.

A large part of everything we have and everything we are comes from those primary groups on which our lives and success depend. Think of the great benefits we get from the company we represent, from our country, from our family, and especially from the Lord. Why shouldn't we contribute in proportion? The more strength we contribute, the more power we receive in return. When we work to make our society strong, then we become strong automatically. No man would be tolerated on a baseball team who was a discredit to the uniform. The tradition and spirit of a great ball club must be in his blood. Every player must be able to depend on the loyalty, support, ability, and stimulation of every other player, for a chain is no stronger than its weakest link. How unfortunate, in our age of wonders and enlightenment when we have been assigned to prepare the earth for the glorious second coming of Christ, to have young people put on the uniform of rebellion and become obsessed with the idea of overthrowing the government, tearing down the establishment, and denying the finest traditions of our culture. We must keep ourselves loyal and devoted to life's highest and most constructive purposes.

Our Pledge of Allegiance, our oath of office, our marriage covenants, our commitments to God, and our obligations to the social order in which we live should not allow for any disloyalty, inconstancy, incompetence, laziness, or mental or moral unfitness.

We should be very proud of our history, and from every individual field of battle we should come off victoriously and honorably. Fear should never be allowed to sit in the councils of our souls. There should be no cringing in us, no dodging of responsibility, but a willingness to go forward with great ability and courage.

When one joins the Church, he takes certain vows; when one assumes the responsibility of a physician, he subscribes to the Hippocratic Oath; when one assumes great political responsibility, he takes the oath of office; when one puts on the uniform of his country, he takes the Pledge of Allegiance. And when one aspires to the glories of eternity, he lives by the laws of righteousness and becomes a part of its symbols. He is now invested with the highest insignia, and he is responsible for its reputation. We should not only be good citizens, good family members, good church members, or good businessmen. Above all, we should be good people.

46 The Laws of TEACHING

A good leader or parent or missionary is also a good teacher. One of our greatest ideas is that understanding can be communicated; excellence can be taught and faith can be developed. No matter what his occupation may be, everyone should understand the learning process. One of the greatest responsibilities of our lives is to teach the gospel of Jesus Christ to everyone.

So far as I know, all teaching success may be attributed to two factors: First, if the teacher understands the tremendous importance of the message that he bears, he is already halfway toward success; and second, if he can understand the tremendous importance of the messenger who bears the message, his efforts will be crowned with greater accomplishment. It is impossible to deliver a great message without a great messenger.

In discharging our obligations to our life's work, we ought to thoroughly understand three laws of teaching, which are:

1. Recency
2. Frequency
3. Intensity

1. *Recency*

All success is accumulative. We acquire knowledge, build up love, or generate convictions a little bit at a time.

One may be very interested in the idea of religion, truth, and righteousness when it is first presented to him, but if he leaves it out of his mind for a period of time, some of the main causes for enthusiasm may grow a little dim. The importance of the message to him may lose some of its luster; he forgets what it will do for him; and his interest in it wanes.

Every person is more or less like a storage battery that needs to be recharged once in a while. It is one of the laws of learning that the freshness of our memories is in proportion to the recency of the impression. A recent presentation has the most power. Therefore, a teacher shouldn't let his learners' convictions get too cold before he follows up by adding a little more enthusiasm and gives more recency to his convictions.

2. *Frequency*

We are told that each time a thought goes through the brain, it makes an imprint, and when the same idea and the same thought goes over the same path several times, the imprint becomes a groove and then a good wide path that can be followed more or less automatically. For example, in the process of building up their faith, a good missionary will call on his investigators frequently. He will see to it that they attend church, sing the great hymns, offer some fervent prayers, and give frequency to their communications with the Spirit.

If a person were to drive his automobile only once a year, he would find that the lubrication has dried up, the battery has gone dead, and the tires have gone flat. The effectively performing automobile is one that is operated every day with regular frequency, and the effectively performing convert is one who regularly follows his religious devotions. Then his religious brain path will be deep and wide and his Christianity will always be fresh and powerful to serve his best interests. There should be a constant reselling job taking place every day with the learner's objective focus centered on truth and righteousness.

Just as we don't usually adopt new ideas or philosophies all at once, so we can't expect that a learner's whole life is going to change as a consequence of a statement made once or an enthusiasm that is felt only once. We develop philosophies, emotions, and habits gradually, and if we give great frequency to teaching religious principles and build up others' enthusiasm, develop their confidence, stimulate their understanding, and motivate them to regular action, we can help them develop into outstanding disciples of the Master.

3. *Intensity*

There are many ways that our teaching and learning may become more vital and impressive. The words of some teachers, some parents, and some missionaries are very effective, while the words of others go like water off a duck's back. What makes the difference? It is possible that there are a number of contributing factors:

a. The conviction of the leader or the teacher or the messenger. It has been said that that which we do not sufficiently believe we cannot adequately say. True conviction is contagious.

b. We can make the presentation live by making it clear, using the illustrations and human interest stories fitted to the subject's needs. We understand most easily those things that come within the realm of our own experience, and in our teaching we should be certain that the learner understands clearly what we're talking about and accepts the idea. The continuity and subject matter of our presentation should be interesting, well organized, and effectively given.

c. The words themselves making up our presentation should be well chosen, colorful, and full of meaning.

d. The place and the atmosphere for the presentation should be as conducive to success as possible. A salesman may not be particularly effective if he tries to make a sale while his prospect is running to catch an airplane. It will be far more effective if he can have the prospect's undivided attention in a place of quiet under the right circumstances. Ideas will then be more impressive and change the learner more permanently.

If we have a great message, it is possible to make the message so intense that the ideas will always remain with the student and cause him to take favorable action upon it.

It is thrilling to think that with great ideas and a great leader following the laws of teaching, we can help people to think, feel, and act in paths that we mark out for them. In planning to make yourself a more effective human being, remember that the laws of teaching and learning are:

Recency
Frequency
Intensity

47 The Law of TRIFLES

Henry Ford once said, "There are no big problems." Life is made up of a lot of little problems that, when taken together, make up large problems. Henry Ford knew how to take a great big problem and divide it into its parts so that each became small enough that he could handle it effectively. The earth itself is made up of a lot of grains of sand. The mighty Niagara Falls is just a lot of drops of water that have all come together in one place. Follow any river to its source and you'll find only a bubble. Napoleon said, "In affairs of magnitude, I have learned that in the last resort everything invariably turns upon a trifle."

The greatest prizes go to the one who knows how to handle little problems. In military achievement, there is a stratagem that says, "Divide and conquer." That is, we should segregate the opposition into units small enough that we can handle them one at a time. Even the largest problems are a combination of little problems, so we need to divide and conquer.

These little units are the tremendous trifles that we have heard about. Success often eludes us because we wait for our big moment to arrive. We wait for some big problem to be solved, going through life expecting a great opportunity that never arrives, and all the time we tread beneath our feet those little opportunities which, if properly handled, would have guaranteed a magnificent success.

For example, suppose you are a young man and want to be a great athlete. Epictetus gives the answer. He said: "You fain would be a victor at the Olympic Games. You should first weigh the conditions. Then after you have made up your mind, lay to your hand. You must live by the rules, submit to diet, abstain from dainty meats, exercise your body at stated hours in heat or in cold, drink no cold water, nor wine. In a word, surrender yourself wholly to your trainer in these little things as you would to a physician. Then in the hour of contest you must be willing to pay the price. If you dislocate an arm, or sprain an ankle, or gulp down an abundance of yellow dust, that is a part of the risk you run. But even after all of this, you may many times lose the victory. But you must never lose heart. So count the cost, and then if your desire still holds, stick to the path of conquering the little things."

Being a champion is made up of a lot of little things. We recall the story of the woman who heard and admired the music of a great violinist. She said, "I would give half my life to be able to play like that." He said, "Madam, that is exactly what I have given." And that is what everyone must give who wishes to be a great violinist. There are many people who would give half their lives to be great violinists but they are not willing to take violin lessons and devote the necessary time to practice.

Many years ago, I attended a national sales convention. Present at this meeting and taking part on the program were some of the greatest salesmen in the world who were there to give the secrets of their success to a group of specially invited delegates. At this convention I learned a lesson that has since been of inestimable value to me. At one of the meetings, I thought of one of my associates who was also attending this convention at the expense of his company. I thought how tremendously he must have been enjoying this feast of proven sales procedures and ideas. But when I looked around to try to locate him, I discovered to my horror that he was not even in the convention hall. I later learned that he had rented a sailboat and was out on the Atlantic Ocean sailing his boat. Then I counted those present, and fewer than one-half of the qualified delegates were absent. Just think of it—here was a group of men who were trying to learn a great business, whose companies had paid their full expenses so they could learn the principles of success. But, like the lady who didn't take violin lessons, these men who were making their living as salesmen didn't even listen to the greatest authorities on their own business.

I have since learned quite a little bit about how this kind of person thinks. He thinks these are little matters, and what difference does it make if he misses a few meetings or a few ideas? Such persons have ways of rationalizing and excusing themselves so that they destroy their success in order to enjoy some whim or fancy of the moment. They exercise bad judgment, weakness, and failure and miss their world, so to speak, because they sidestepped the little grains of sand of which it was made up.

Even the greatest tree grows an imperceptible amount each day, but every little bit counts, and the tree that keeps growing steadily eventually becomes a giant. In researching this idea a little bit, I found one man who was at the top in sales work who told me that in his twenty-six years of attending his company's national sales conventions, he had never missed a single meeting to which he had been invited nor had he ever been late on one occasion—for the simple reason that he could not afford to. If we miss just one day's growth, that is a day that is completely lost, and we can never make it up.

Suppose we try to think of all the things that make up success. We probably cannot think of any of them that are very large in themselves. One of the most striking characteristics of the life of Socrates was that he never allowed himself to become heated in a discussion. He never uttered an injurious or insulting word. That is a little thing, but think how important it is when put in a character constellation with a hundred other little things.

Socrates further said, "Whatsoever place you assign me, sooner I will die a thousand times than desert it." One cannot imagine Socrates taking money from his country or his company for the purpose of improving himself and then spending his time sailing a boat while the intellectual and occupational fireworks are taking place. He would probably not want to miss one word that was spoken or one bit of the enthusiasm that pervades an assemblage of the finest talent that he himself was trying to develop. Socrates said, "One man finds pleasure in improving his land, another his horses; my pleasure is in seeing that I myself grow better day by day."

Marriage is made up of a lot of little courtesies and kindnesses. Again we might make up a list of the tremendous trifles that would stop the carnage of divorce and lift our lives above the commonplace.

Here's a contribution from Demosthenes: "The chief part of an orator is *action;* the next part is *action;* the third is *action.*" That is so simple that we turn up our noses—but still, it's the recipe for being an orator, and we may take it or leave it.

We learn to do by doing. We get skill into our muscles by taking action on great ideas. Everyone wants to command the end of success, but few people are willing to endure the means that lead to it. Many people want to be great violinists, but only a comparative few are willing to take violin lessons. We want to go to the top of the occupational and social lists, but we so frequently fail to develop the industry or the enthusiasm that will get us there. Many of us are full of a lot of little leaks, each so small that we think them of no consequence, and yet they prevent us from obtaining great total stature.

The milky way is comprised of a lot of little stars compounding their light. The mold of man's fortune is in little things. Reading a good book occasionally may seem a little thing, but books contain the potency of life in them, as active as was the soul whose progeny they are. Books preserve for us, as in a vial, the purest concentrate of that living intellect which bred them.

Think of the little things that made Mahatma Gandhi the unquestioned leader of 500,000,000 people. He said, "I hold that a man that deliberately and knowingly takes and breaks a pledge forfeits his manhood." Gandhi's greatness lay in doing what everybody *could* do, but didn't. His secret was action. He did not attempt to be clever. Once he declared, "I have never had recourse to cunning in all my life." Face-saving was to him an unknown concept.

The law says that the things that make us are little

things and the things that trip us up are about the same size. We step on a little banana peel; we take a little pleasant poison; Eve ate a little apple. If we would be a success, we must learn the power of the law of trifles. No problems are as big as we are, but if there is a question, we should take it apart and solve it a little bit at a time.

48 The Law of VISION

One of the most thrilling stories in the New Testament tells of a blind man named Bartimaeus who begged for his living by the roadside just outside the city of Jericho. When he heard that Jesus of Nazareth was about to pass by, he began calling to him. Jesus heard Bartimaeus and asked that he be brought. Then Jesus said to him, "What wilt thou that I should do unto thee?" The blind man had asked for many things from many people as they had come down this road from Jericho, probably none of which had any great value. But this time he didn't ask for some small thing. When Jesus said, "What wilt thou that I should do unto thee," Bartimaeus replied, "Lord, that I might receive my sight." (See Mark 10:46-52.)

That is the thing we need more than anything else in the world. We need vision; we need understanding; we need appreciation. We don't see far enough, clearly enough, or soon enough.

Vision, the ability to see, is usually thought of as being a physical quality, but eyes are merely the instruments of sight. Sight itself is in our judgment, our understanding, our imagination. There are many things in a mountain range, for example, that may be visible to a geologist but that would remain unseen to one whose mind lacks the necessary knowledge or vision. One of the most common of experiences is to meet those "who have eyes but see not."

Vision probably has its most important aspect when we think of it as a quality of personality. Few people can look objectively and clearly beyond the boundary of their present circumstances. If an automobile could shine its light only one foot ahead of the radiator cap, a crack-up might reasonably be expected on a dark road at night. Such shortness of vision in human beings gives the same promise of trouble ahead. One of the greatest elements of safety in human personality, therefore, is that ability to look and plan ahead, and the value of this quality is in proportion to the clearness of the visibility and the range of the vision.

Many people are severely handicapped by shortsightedness. This not only jeopardizes security but also impairs usefulness and limits success. Many otherwise capable people are unable to look ahead or contemplate those future circumstances that come outside their own experiences or the circle of their present needs. When one has his eyes focused too much on the present, the future tends to be blotted out of the vision. The story is told of the man who sold his bed of straw in the morning and then came back in the evening tearfully pleading to get it back, not having foreseen that he would need it again.

Vision causes some of the greatest differences between people. The person who has vision thinks about and prepares for the future, while the person who lacks vision lives each day as it comes. One of the differences between humans and animals is that animals live only in the present. They walk on all fours with their eyes usually directed to the ground. Their vision is confined to a horizon of a few paces. By contrast, a human being stands upright in the image of his Maker so that he might look up to God and righteousness and eternal life. Our vision may reach the stars and bring back to us all the beauty and harmony of the universe.

Shortsightedness is usually caused by being more interested than we should be in the present. This quality makes us like children, to whom the quarter today seems more important than the dollar tomorrow. It was shortsightedness that made Esau trade his birthright for a mess of pottage. It is a shortsighted medical student who, in planning his financial future, says, "Don't tell me what I'm going to be able to earn in five or ten years from now—I am interested only in what I get today." Of course, such a person should never go to medical school in the first place or do any other thing that a far sighted man would know was necessary.

The old maxim still applies that "where there is no vision, the people perish." We should develop the ability to project our plans and hopes beyond the boundary of our present circumstances.

One of the functions of the imagination is to help us transport ourselves into the future so that we can prelive events before we actually experience them. We can anticipate marriage, business opportunities, family situations, an improved personality, death, and even eternal life. The imagination compounds and mixes our own experience with the experiences of others and adds reason, hope, and faith to give us a picture of our future. This combination of virtues adds up to give us vision.

By virtue of our knowledge and good judgment, we can develop faith in our imagination until we have the actual experience. Imagination is one of the main ingredients of vision. The greatest areas of pleasure and pain, hopes and fears, both present and future, come by reason of our ability to see ahead. The quality of our vision is enhanced by our taste, the things we hope for, the amount of our industry, and the kind of person that we desire to become.

We can't afford to wait until the event takes place to prepare for it. If one waits to make an investment until all the reports are in and he knows what the profit will be, it may then be too late. In trying to see into the future, we should remember that there is an optical illusion in everybody which makes things close by look large and important, whereas things at a distance look small and insignificant. We have learned to make allowance for this phenomenon so far as physical eyesight is concerned. We are not fooled by the fact that the telephone pole by which we are standing seems very large and the one on the distant horizon seems like a pinpoint by comparison.

One of the advantages that distance has over time is that in distance we can actually traverse the space to the horizon and by actual experience find that the telephone pole on the horizon is not of miniature size. Because this is subject to our experience, we have learned to compensate for it. Effective vision regarding time is when the imagination paints distant objectives so large in our consciousness that they seem to us even more important than the goals of the present. The imagination is capable of running ahead and focusing the spotlight on the future so that it stands out like a beacon to light our way. Vision means light. The more light we can get on the objective, the better.

In the list of personality qualities we need to develop, we ought to include vision. One of the greatest causes of distress in life is shortsightedness. We must learn to look ahead, to think in terms of the future, and to learn to compensate effectively for the illusion that makes distant objects look unimportant. Then when we finally reach the horizon and look back, we will understand that the future has now become the most important of all. Vision says, "I see it." Faith says, "I believe it." Industry says, "I will achieve it."

One of the greatest of all accomplishments is to be able to say, as did the blind man, "Whereas I was blind, now I see."

49 The Law of the WILL

The will has been defined as "the power of conscious, deliberate action, that faculty by which the rational mind makes choices of its ends of actions, and then directs the energies in carrying out its determination." This power to carry out what has been previously determined upon is one of the greatest of all accomplishments.

The will is the executive. It is the boss. It is the determiner of success. The greatest success comes when we learn how to strengthen, organize, and train the will. Of course we do not fully understand this mysterious mental power. Nature has taught us how to use our limbs without giving us the knowledge of the muscles and nerves by which they are actuated. Although nature has planted within us this miraculous power called the will, and although this is the means by which we go forward, yet we are largely ignorant of the very powers and forces on which our action depends.

The command of the mind over itself is frequently more limited than is its command over the body. These limits are known only by experience, not by reason. Our ability to control our sentiments and passions is much weaker than the ability to control ideas, though we do not know why. We know from experience that a man in health possesses more self-command than one languishing in sickness; therefore we should keep ourselves healthy. It is also far easier to will to do something we like than to do something we do not like. Therefore we should train our attitudes so we like good things.

If we keep working vigorously at it, someday we may understand better how to manage ourselves. Mankind did not discover the secrets of blood circulation until the year 1616, and it may be that as we continue to discover ourselves, we will learn something about the development of the greatest of all potential powers, our own will to do and to become.

The power of will includes the power to imagine, to desire, to control and correct. We are more the masters of our thoughts at some times than at other times. Like everything else, will power is strengthened by practice. We discipline our minds and we discipline our actions by making them subject to the higher power of the will. For the person who has developed a very strong will, all things are easy. It is also possible for us to be careless and to allow the will to lose its strength. There are probably few sights more pitiful than a human being who has lost control of himself. There are many people who make New Year's resolutions but do not have the will to follow through. They will one thing but do something else. They formulate great plans, but nothing happens.

One of the qualities that everyone interested in success should strive to develop is the quality of strength in the will. This is the ability to do the things that we plan. It is the power by which we can move the organs of our bodies or direct the faculties of our minds or personalities. An act of volition of the will may produce motion in our limbs or paint a new picture in our imaginations.

One seeking success and happiness should learn to think, but he should also learn to make his thoughts and feelings subject to his will. The highest power in the world is will power. In the power of the will, man shows himself farthest removed from the animal. Animals don't have will power. They don't have reasoning. They are consigned at birth to a life pattern from which they are unable to depart. With man this is not so. It is in the will that "man shows himself most like God."

We should train ourselves to increase the command of the will over the mind and to develop further the authority of the will over the sentiments and passions as well as over the body. The will is an executive, and a good executive organizes and controls. He is dependable. He can always be relied upon. He never fails. He is never behind time. He always brings the ship into port. May we always strive to remember the important law of the will.

50 The Law of WORDS

The painter works with color, the sculptor with form, and the musician with tone. Color and form and tone are beautiful and significant by virtue of what they are able to express, but they all fade into insignificance when compared with the power of speech. This is especially true in occupations in which speech is the instrument by which people also make their living. Automobiles run, airplanes fly, but most men literally talk themselves forward. Words are our most important tools, and one of the most effective ways of achieving success is to learn the meaning and shading and use of words.

A mediocre idea well expressed is often more effective than a better idea poorly expressed. Sir Winston Churchill's great leadership was largely based on his power of speech. Few men have understood the delicacies and luxuries of language better than he did; people read his works not only for what he says but for the way he says it. He met one crisis after another by his ability to express an idea with vivid imagery and tremendous force. These he prepared in advance—some of his neatly turned phrases are too smooth and perfect to be extemporaneous. But why shouldn't he prepare in advance? Napoleon didn't wait until the battle began to mold his cannon balls.

While facts constitute the material out of which arguments are made, yet passions, prejudices, sentiments, and the emotions play a strong part in determining the actions of human beings, and these are addressed, stimulated, and set on fire by the proper combination, shading, and expression of words and meanings.

An unfortunate woman tramped through the empty streets of Paris at dawn one gray autumn day, starvation and despair in her eyes, mechanically tapping her drum and chanting, "Bread, bread, bread." She started the French Revolution in 1789.

Mark Antony took the Roman Empire away from Brutus and his fellow conspirators by the power of the words he uttered at the funeral of Caesar. Lawyers win cases, ministers save souls, statesmen make history, and salesmen make sales by the effective use of words. The quality of the idea and the effectiveness of its expression determine what will happen in the minds of those who listen.

Persons who are engaged in such business as teaching, leading, selling, politics, and other forms of persuasion and motivation ought to read and study logic, debate, rhetoric, literature, drama, language, poetry, all of which have to do with the effective understanding and use of words. Socrates used words to throw his listeners into perfect ecstasies. One who reads poetry must respond to its mood and stretch his mind to its widest dimensions. Great poets have stood next to the prophets in their ability to influence our lives. They have been persons whose imaginations have dared to leave the ground and ascend high enough to enable them to take a broader view of things. By the witchery of its music and radiance of its imagery, poetry gives pleasure to a leisure moment as well as helps us to master the art of word combinations.

The evocative power of words is the secret of the poet. It is the secret of sales motivation. It wins for the lawyer and the politician. It is especially potent when there is added to it the influence of the character of the one who is using the words. Even a nod from a person who is esteemed is of more force than a thousand arguments or studied sentences from others.

It was said that Demosthenes was the best orator of his time, but Phoecian was the most powerful speaker.

Commenting on the effect of these two speakers, when one spoke the people said, "How well Cicero speaks," but when the other spoke, they said, "Let's take up arms against Caesar." Zeno said that a philosopher should never speak until his words have been steeped in meaning.

The force of words can do more than can ever be done by conquering swords. Pyrrhus used to say that Cineas had taken more towns with his words than he had with his arms. It is easy to overcome the bodies of those whose spirits have already been defeated.

It was said of Pericles that he wielded a dreadful thunderbolt from his tongue, and thunder and lightning resulted when he harangued. Others have been said to have such powerful use of words that they cut or hiss or pierce or burn. Words may also be used to soothe and comfort and heal.

The chief business of speech is to address the affections, the passions, the prejudices, and the ideas and feelings of men. What great power there is in the tongue if it is properly trained, especially when it is backed up by the reputation of a life and character free from every kind of corruption and taint.

One experienced sales manager wrote to an agent as follows:

> Dear Agent: John Barrymore is an actor of long experience and great ability. How long would his reputation continue if he spoke extemporaneously and at random instead of giving the same old Hamlet speech that never fails to get across its message? Jane Cowl is one of the best Juliets ever to play the part. She says the same words the thousandth night as she did the first night, and people gladly pay five dollars to hear her. No one has yet succeeded in improving the wording of the Sermon on the Mount or the Gettysburg speech. Robert Ingersoll's address at his brother's grave brings the same emotions today that it did when first spoken. Wellington's appeal to his soldiers before the battle of Waterloo—well, read it. I ask you with all the earnestness at my command to prepare or adopt an already prepared, standardized canvass, one for each type of prospect—say four canvasses in all. They will make you money just as they made money for Jane Cowl and Barrymore and Bryan.

Study the word combinations of men like Winston Churchill. During the Battle of Britain he said, "Let us . . . so bear ourselves that, if the British Empire and its Commonwealth last for a thousand years, men will still say, 'This was their finest hour.' "

Statesmen have achieved greatness by the power and effectiveness of their speech. They are able to dominate and lead the will of their followers by the power of language. To help us develop greater word power, we should read the inspired holy scriptures and memorize the parables of Jesus. Many events live in history not because of the events themselves but because someone has told of the event effectively.

The greatest weapons men have are the weapons of their speech. Someone has said, "The pen is mightier than the sword." We carry on the contest for success with the weapon with which we should excel, our speech. Words effectively used are the magic carpet on which we fly to success.

INDEX

A

Abraham, 7
Abundance, 13-18
Achilles, 82
Acquisition, instinct for, 133
Adult, childishness, 145
Advantage, law of, 19-21
Adversity, 178
Age, chronological and emotional, 144
Aintree Steeplechase, 121
Alexander the Great, 79, 143
Allergy to roses, story about, 50
Ambition, 61, 185
Antony, Mark, 211
Apelles, 81
Apostle Paul, 150
Appearance and grooming, 61
Appreciation, 22-25
Approval, desire for, 59, 133
Arabian sheik, story about, 74
Arctic Circle, aviator in, 118
Aristotle, 79
Arnold, Benedict, 51
Arrested development, 26-30
Averages, law of, 161-65
Aviator in Arctic Circle, 118

B

Babylonian empire, 8
Barrymore, John, 212
Bartimaeus, 203
Baseball, victory in, 189
Battle of Britain, 187, 213
Beans and walnuts, illustration of, 123
Benet, Stanford, 144
Blessings, how to receive, 40-41
Blind man healed by Jesus, 203
Blindness, 203-206
Boomerang, law of, 31-33
Borrowing, 95
Bradford, Gamaliel, 51, 174
Brain, composition of, 131
Brooklyn, 189
Burbank, Luther, 7

C

Caesar, Julius, 16, 57, 141
Capitalistic system, 101
Carlyle, Thomas, 78
Carnegie, Andrew, 109
Cato, 80, 174
Celestial kingdom, 152
Champion, how to be, 199
Chance, 34-36
Chance World, The, 35
Character, 103
Charles I, 78
Checkup, 172
Cherry trees, illustration about, 182
Childishness, 146
Church is divine institution, 2
Church work, compensation in, 40-42
Churchill, Sir Winston, 210, 213
Cicero, 212
Cineas, 212
Clouds, signs in, 169
Columbus, 192
Combative instincts, 133
Commandments of God, keeping, 151

Community responsibility, 96-97
Compartmentalization of personality, 185-86
Compensation, 37
Concentration, 43-47
Conditioned responses, 48-50
Consequences, 51-54
Constitution of the United States, 2
Convention, delegates at, 199-200
Conversion, 162, 164
Council of heaven, 9, 152
Courage, 55-58
Covenants, 193
Credit, 96; dangers of, 95
Crime in the world, 87-88
Criticism, 175
Curiosity, instinct for, 133

D

Damaged Souls (book), 51, 174
Death of young man, 168
Demosthenes, 201, 211
Details, too much concern with, 46
Determination, 124
Development, arrested, 26-30
Dickens, Charles, 73
Disease, a fractional death, 120
Disloyalty, 141
Disobedience, 119
Disraeli, Benjamin, 137
Distortion, 71
Dogmatic statements, 159
Dreaming, 147
Dyer, Edward, poem by, 150

E

Ederle, Gertrude, 153
Edison, Thomas A., 7, 43, 86, 150
Ego recognition, 59-62
Einstein, 7, 86
Elegance, 63-66
Emerson, Ralph Waldo, 15, 38, 39, 44
Emotional control, 127
Emotional health, 117
Emotions, stable, 125
Enemies, learning to love, 31-32; love our, 137
England, system of government in, 78; horse race in, 121
English Channel, 153
Epictetus, 198
Eternal exaltation, 163
Evidence, law of, 67-71
Exaggeration, 72-77
Example, 78-83
Excellence, 66
Expediency, 70
Experience, 84-88; learning from, 132

F

Facts, rules governing, 67, 69-70
Failure, reasons for, 17
Family success, 75
Farragut, Admiral, 91
Fatigue, 130, 133
Faults, overlooking, 106
Fear, 89-93; instinct for, 133, 134
Finances, in the home, 97-98
Financial respectability, 94-99
Firmness, 160
Follow-up, 172
Ford, Henry, 7, 86, 150, 198
Franklin, Benjamin, 5, 158
Free agency, 100-102
Freedom, 87; of religion, 1-2
Freedoms, alternatives to, 102
French Revolution, 211
Frequency in teaching, 195-96
Freud, Sigmund, 27, 119
Friendship, 138
Fusion, law of, 103-104

G

Galileo, 5
Gandhi, Mohandas K., 186-88, 201
Garfield, James A., 91
Genuineness, 64
Glad tidings, 105-108
Goals, 153-57
God, is supreme lawgiver, 7-8
Goddess of beauty, 81
Goebbels, Paul Joseph, 50
Golden Rule, 31, 33
Good news, reward to bearer of, 105
Gospel, meaning of, 107
Government, role of, 1-2, 3
Grand National Steeplechase, 121
Gratitude, 22
Gravity-up, law of, 109-112
Gray, Albert E.N., 155
Growth, 113-15; stages of, 27

H

Hale, Nathan, 141
Hamlet, 53

Hammurabi, 8
Happiness, 76, 208; eternal, 107
Harmon, Tom, 58
Health, 116-120
Heredity, 148
Higgins, Professor Henry, 137
Hippocrates, 7
Hippocratic Oath, 193
Hitler, Adolph, 50, 68
Holy Grail, 74
Homer, 82
Horse, boy thrown from, 28
How Old Am I Financially? (booklet), 94
Hubbard, Elbert, 141, 183, 191
Human nature, 105
Humor, sense of, 20
Hunger pangs, 133
Hur, Ben, 37-38, 42
Hurdle, law of, 121-24
Hypochondria, 125-27

I

Idleness, 128-30
Ignorance, 91
Imagination, 73, 87, 157, 205, 208; distorted, 180
Imitate, instinct to, 133
Immaturity, 30, 31, 144-48
Immortality and eternal life, 41
India, 187
Inertia, 61, 114, 185
Inferiority complex, 169
Instincts, 85, 131-34
Integrity, 187; financial, 95-96
Intensity in teaching, 196
Inventions, modern, 19
"Invictus" (poem), 178

J

James, Jesse, 175
James, William, 49, 66
Jekyll, Dr., and Mr. Hyde, 185
Jesus Christ, 150, 203; was greatest lawgiver, 9; description of resurrected, 65
Judas, betrayal of Christ by, 23
Judgment, 205; sound, 167

K

Kepler, 5
King David, 150-51
King John, by Shakespeare, 56
King Phillip, 79
Knowledge, 145, 205

L

Labor-saving devices, 39
Launfal, Sir, 74
Laws, forces against, 3; reasons for, 4; obedience to, 4-5; commitment to, 11-12; undeviating, 36
Lawyer, role of, 10
Laziness, 91
Learning, 194-97
Life expectancy, 162
Life insurance protection, 96
Lincoln, Abraham, 16, 86, 111, 138
Locks, on great waterways, 19-20
Love, 135-39; instinct for, 133
Loyalty, 140-43
Lucifer, 152; rebellion of, 9

M

Macbeth, Lady, 53, 126-27
Magnetism, 110, 111
Magnets, 154; electric, 110
Managers, 182
Mantle, Mickey, 189
Marcus Aurelius, 82
Marriage, 191, 201; problems in, 136
Massachusetts School for the Blind, 122
Maturity, 144-48
Maxim, Roman emperor, 154
Meissonier, 62
Menninger, Dr. Karl, 117
Mental breakdown, 178
Mental health, 125-26
Mental illness, 117, 119
Mental inertia, 128
Military uniform, importance of, 190
Milton, John, 16, 73
Mind, command over, 207
Missionary work, 41-42, 162, 164
Modification, 149-52
Morality, 164
Mortality, 149
Moses, was great lawgiver, 9
Motivation, 111

N

Napoleon, 16, 137, 155-56, 175, 210
Nature, resources in, 13-14
New York Yankees, 189

Newton, Isaac, 5, 109
Niagara Falls, 198

O

Oaths, 193
Objectives, 153-57
Objectivity, 71
Obstacles, 122, 130; overcoming, 113
Olympic Games, 199
Opposites, 101
Organization, 188
Ostrich, 173
Overbearing attitude, 159

P

Parental instinct, 133
Parlette, Ralph, 123
Patriotism, 142
Pavlov, Ivan, 48
Pearl Harbor, 90
Peers, rule by, 78-79
Penitentiary, man sentenced to, 53
Pericles, 80, 212
Personal relations, 61
Personality, research on, 30; acquired, 55; qualities, 103
Phoecian, 211
Physical grooming, 64
Pity for others, 179
Planning, 171
Plato, 82
Pledge of Allegiance, 193
Plutarch, 15, 80, 82
Positive statements, 158-60
Positiveness, 160
Power steering, 170
Preparation for meeting needs, 90
Priesthood, robes of, 191
Probability, 161-65
Problems, solving, 113
Productiveness, 182
Psychiatry, science of, 26-27
Psychosomatic medicine, 117
Punishments, 52
Pygmalion and Galatea, 135
Pyrrhus, 212

R

Raleigh, Sir Walter, 14
Reason, 166-69
Recency in teaching, 194-95
Recognition, need for, 23
Record keeping, 163
Religion, freedom of, 1-2
Repentance, 75
Reputation, 21, 103
Reserve, financial, 96
Resources, natural, 13-14
Restlessness, 114
Retaliation, 31
Righteousness, 119
Rogers, Will, 138
Roman Empire, 211

S

Sabbath day, 41, 65
Salesmanship, 10, 34-35, 162, 163, 199
Schizophrenia, 185
Second childhood, 147
Self-analysis, 104
Self-control, 170-72
Self-deception, 173-77
Self-pity, 178-80
Self-preservation, 62; instinct for, 133
Self-supervision, 181-84
Senses, power of, 21
Sex instinct, 133
Shakespeare, William, 80-81, 93, 150
Shaw, George Bernard, 137
Ship, sinking, captain of, 140
Shortsightedness, 204
Signs in clouds, 169
Singleness of purpose, 45
Smile, importance of, 21
Socrates, 82, 200
Solitude, 176
Solomon, 91, 150-51
Southwell, Robert, 135
Spartans, 81
Speaking, public, 166
Speech, 212; importance of, 63-64
Split personality, 185-88
Statesmanship, 213
Stevenson, Robert Louis, 62
Stimulants, mental and spiritual, 115
Struggle, benefits of, 113-14
Success, 86
Sunflower, 140
Supervision, 181
Supervisors, 182

T

Teaching, 194-97
Temperature controls of body, 131
Temptation, meaning of, 110

Ten Commandments, 9
Tennyson, Alfred, Lord, 74, 149
Thesis, writing of, 10-11
Thinking, positive, 15-16, 17
"Three Friends Have I" (poem), 139
Tithing, 40-41
Trifles, 198-202
Truth, 68

U

Uniform, symbolism of, 189-92
University of Michigan, 58

V

Valley Forge, 16
Vices, 92
Violinist, becoming great, 199
Vision, 203-206
Vivisection, 176

W

Washington, George, 9, 16, 86, 162
Weaknesses, 86
Whitman, Walt, 17, 49
Whittier, John Greenleaf, 109
Will of deceased man, 156
Will-power, 207-209
Words, 210-12
Work, 182-84; freedom in, 100
World Series, 189
Wright Brothers, 7

Y

Young, Brigham, 126

Z

Zeno, 80, 212